658.45 K
Communic
  effecti
35000094
MAIN

D0069771

Garry Kranz is a freelance writer with a twenty-year career in journalism. His articles have won numerous regional awards for spot reporting and feature writing. He is a contributor to several national publications, writing about high technology, nanotechnology, human resources, economic development, and how politics affect business. During his many years in the workforce, he has made dozens of presentations, made thousands of phone calls, and written more than one million business e-mails.

Contents

Preface

How do you write effective e-mails? What can you do to make your reports more persuasive? If you have an important message to communicate to a colleague in Germany, should you adopt a casual or formal tone? When is it okay to instant message at work? How should you prepare a presentation? Why is it important to watch for nonverbal cues when talking with your boss, employees, or colleagues?

In this book, we distill the wisdom of some of the best minds in the field of business communication to tell you how to communicate effectively. The language is simple and the design colorful to make the information easy to grasp.

Quizzes help you assess your knowledge of communication issues. Case files show how people have addressed their own communication challenges. Sidebars give you a big-picture look at how to deliver your message more clearly and highlight innovative, out-of-the-box solutions worth considering (e.g., e-mail-free Fridays, anyone?). Quotes from business leaders and writing and communications experts will inspire you as you face your daily barrage of meetings, difficult conversations, e-mails, memos, reports, and letters. Finally, in case you want to dig deeper into the topic of communication and management, we recommend some of the most important business books available. The authors of these books both influence and reflect today's thinking about communicating effectively and related management issues. Understanding the ideas they cover will inspire you as a manager.

Even if you don't dip into these volumes, the knowledge you gain from studying the pages of this book will equip you with the right tools to communicate clearly every day—to help you make a difference to your company and the lives of the people who support you.

THE EDITORS

COMMUNICATING CLEARLY IN WRITING

"You can have brilliant ideas, but if you can't get them across, your ideas won't get you anywhere."

—Lee Iacocca,
former CEO of Chrysler

What is your game plan, and does your team know it? Just like a coach in sports, you as manager are charged with guiding a team of individuals toward its collective goal. Successful execution depends on your capacity to communicate this game plan clearly.

You need to be sure all team members read from the same playbook. Each player's role and responsibilities must be meticulously defined. The coaching and instruction you give must be delivered accurately and with the right timing. Nothing good happens if communication falters. A championship-caliber game plan is worthless if the coach sends the wrong signals to the players.

If you are reading this book to improve your ability to communicate, you obviously see the link between strong communication skills and career success. In this book you will find advice for developing your own "communications playbook." It is not intended to be exhaustive, and its aim is simple: to provide digestible bites of information to help you gain confidence and master the art of both written and oral communication. No matter how high-tech and diverse communication technologies become, they can reach their full potential only when used by a good writer or speaker.

THE BASICS OF COMMUNICATING IN WRITING

The need to write clearly and thoughtfully arises in virtually every situation you face as a manager. Good writing, in fact, is one of the most highly prized competencies. An e-mail, memo, letter, or formal report each has its own special requirements, but fundamental principles apply to all business writing: planning before writing, using correct grammar, knowing your audience, understanding the purpose of your writing, striking the right tone, and revising and editing.

Research and Planning

Before you start writing, gather all the information required to craft an effective message. Consult whatever business intelligence you will need—such as sales forecasts, customer history, industry trends, and other applicable information—so you can back up your statements directly in your correspondence or report. For weighty matters, you may need to do more extensive research to buttress the points you intend to make.

> "Think before you write. Nothing worthwhile yields to human effort without a plan."
>
> —L. E. Frailey,
> author of *Handbook of Business Letters*

Whether research is needed depends greatly on your subject and the people to whom you are writing. Doing research at a library or performing a detailed search using the Internet is usually sufficient to back up your points with hard facts. In communications within a department or organization, such research may be unnecessary. But supporting your correspondence or sales materials to prospective customers with relevant business information helps win their confidence and can help generate new business.

Before you write, map out the information you plan to share and why you are doing so. Start by jotting down notes on paper and then highlighting the key issues you want to emphasize.

Dos & Don'ts ☑

NOTE-TAKING BASICS

Distilling the most important information from a mass of material is easier if you work efficiently and deliberately. Here are some pointers:

☐ Don't frustrate yourself with excessive research.

☐ Do jot down only the most pertinent information.

☐ Don't write sloppily and assume you will be able to read your handwriting later.

☐ Don't write complete sentences while taking notes (unless needed for clarification). Instead, jot down phrases.

☐ Do use abbreviations, as long as you can understand them. Example: "$3K" instead of "3,000 dollars."

☐ Do write special comments in the margins for later reference.

The note-taking process is helpful in two ways. First, the act of writing itself tends to stimulate ideas or concepts you had not previously considered—scholars call this "emergent information." Second, seeing ideas in front of you makes it easier to sort out the most essential details and organize them in a logical order. Keep similar items and ideas together. This will help you recognize repetition or determine in what form the information can best be communicated.

Grammar, Language, and Style

Regardless of the form in which you are writing—say, a casual e-mail, a formal letter, or a report—you should always aim to write with clarity and simplicity. For example, rather than writing that your company is "interested in aligning the potentialities of your company with our long-standing reputation as a global innovator," write that your company "has a strong reputation as an innovator. We should discuss how we can benefit each other by joining forces."

In writing, less is often more—keep it short and to the point. Always use correct grammar and accurate language. If you feel this is one of your weak areas, keep a standard grammar and style book such as *The Elements of Style* by William Strunk, Jr. and E. B. White by your desk.

Rules of grammar and writing were developed so that we could all understand one another. In contexts where accurate and respectful communication is important, these rules can assume greater weight than they do in day-to-day affairs. Some people are sticklers for minutiae when reading business correspondence. Here are some of the most common mistakes writers make:

Wrong use of contractions. "It's" is a contraction for "it is." "Its" (no apostrophe) indicates the possessive case of the impersonal pronoun. For example:

> The hotline number is now operating. Its purpose is to provide better communication with our customers. It's imperative that all messages left on the hotline be answered within one business day.

The contraction "they're" and the plural possessive "their" are also often used incorrectly. The following example illustrates the misuses of "it's" and "they're":

> The company is sending out it's orders today. Customers should receive they're orders next week.

> Written correctly:

> The company is sending out its orders today. Customers should receive their orders next week.

Overuse of commas and comma splicing. Commas can be used as pauses between major ideas in sentences. If possible, keep them to a minimum. Also, do not string or splice together complete sentences with only a comma when a logical connecting word or phrase is needed. "I think, I am" is a comma splice. The missing word makes all the difference: "I think, therefore I am."

Failure to hyphenate properly. A "small business problem" is quite different from a "small-business problem." Written without hyphens, the phrase would not be clear. Is the problem a small one or is it one typically found in small businesses? In general, two nouns used together to modify another noun are hyphenated (for example, time-management skills).

Less versus fewer. Use "less" for entities that are difficult or impossible to count—snow, rain,

---

LESS IS MORE

General Anthony Clement McAuliffe was commander of division artillery of the 101st Airborne Division during World War II. During the Battle of the Bulge, the Germans had surrounded McAuliffe's paratroopers and demanded that he surrender immediately. Unperturbed, McAuliffe communicated his refusal to the German high command in a one-word response: "Nuts."

The retort has become the stuff of legend. It also contains a powerful communication lesson for managers: Less is often more.

THE BOTTOM LINE

time, money. Use "fewer" for terms that *can* be counted—meetings, managers, machines. Keep in mind these particular correct usages: "We spent less money this month" and "the newer machines take fewer coins."

> "The difference between the right word and the almost right word is really a large matter— 'tis the difference between the lightning bug and the lightning."
>
> —Mark Twain,
> American author
> (1835–1910)

Which versus that. These two words introduce a clause that describes a noun. Using "that" indicates the clause is "essential"; it is vital to the sentence's meaning, providing specific information. For example, "The memo that addresses purchase orders needs to be sent today." But introducing the clause with "which," offset by commas, indicates the clause is "nonessential."

For example, "The memo, which addresses purchase orders, needs to be sent today." In this sentence, the nonessential clause "which addresses purchase orders" could be deleted without losing the point of the sentence: "The memo needs to be sent today."

Redundancies are redundant. All history is past history. All completions are finalized.

Some phrases make no sense when you think about them, or they mean something that was never intended. How often have you read that a "first annual" golf tournament was being held? If the event is intended to be annual, say so. Until it has actually become a yearly occurrence, however, use "first-ever," "inaugural," or "debut" instead. Also beware of "close proximity." By definition, two businesses in "proximity" to each other are nearby; "close proximity" suggests that they are even closer.

Write for Your Audience

Try putting yourself in the shoes of the readers to whom you are directing your message. How will they react to the information? What information do they care most about? What do they need from you?

Knowing your audience will also help you determine the degree of formality with which you should write. For example, though contractions such as "I'll" or "we'll" were once considered casual shorthand for the proper terms "I shall," "I will," "we shall," or "we will," formal business writing no longer frowns upon their use. Although there are no hard-and-fast rules on using casual contractions, knowing who you are writing for should dictate whether to use them or not. If you are unsure, always err on the side of caution and avoid contractions and other less-formal conventions. Keep the stamp of professionalism uppermost in your mind.

In today's global economy, with more and more companies outsourcing parts of their business functions to firms in other countries, communicating with colleagues and customers outside the United States has become common. When writing to an international business

Dos & Don'ts ☑

WRITING FOR AN AUDIENCE

Keeping your audience in mind means being aware of and addressing their particular concerns.

☐ Do orient your message around the reader's interests.

☐ Do determine the level of formality based on your audience.

☐ Do maintain a professional tone, even in less formal writing.

☐ Don't forget to take cultural and language differences into consideration.

☐ Do invite readers to respond.

audience, be mindful that they tend to prefer more formal communications. For example, refrain from addressing overseas business contacts by their first names unless instructed otherwise; always use their full names, or address them by title and last name ("Ms. Jones," "Mr. Smith").

Writing with a Purpose

Once you have a clear understanding of who your audience is, you need to answer the question: Why am I writing?

You may be writing an e-mail to ask an employee or coworker for information. Or you might be writing a report to convince your boss that increasing resources is necessary to complete a project on time. Figuring out the purpose of your communication will help you organize your writing, assess what kind of evidence or information you need to back up your statements, and determine the style and tone of your writing.

In general, most written business communications have one of two purposes: to request information or the resolution of an issue, or to persuade.

Writing to request or resolve. Open with a respectful greeting to the person you are addressing before quickly moving on to the purpose of the request. If you don't know the proper contact name, make a quick telephone call to find it out, rather than using the generic "To whom it may concern."

State the specific reason for writing in the first sentence of your document or letter. Be sure to supply identifying information of special relevance to your reader—a reference to a previous conversation or event, a document, customer order, invoice, or job number, etc. This gives context to your message and enables a reader to be reasonably assured it is valid, especially if you are contacting someone for the first time.

If you are hoping to resolve an issue, avoid sarcasm and accusations. Not only do you risk letting anger cloud your judgment, but you will not endear yourself to the very people who could solve your problem. If you do feel the need to express your dissatisfaction, use a civil tone and address the person respectfully. When sending an e-mail, keep in mind that it is a medium in which the tone of a message can be easily misinterpreted as sarcasm or disrespect.

Writing to persuade. Trying to get someone to come around to your way of thinking is never easy. It is decidedly more difficult using only the written word, which cannot communicate facial expressions or the inflections of voice that lend emphasis during a conversation. Nevertheless, crafting a convincing correspondence or report is possible. Your power of persuasion will be determined largely by your selection of words.

When crafting a persuasive message, experts say, one word is more powerful than all others: "You." Don't begin by talking about yourself. Instead, let the person on the receiving end take center stage. Connect your purpose in writing with the interests and needs of your reader.

For example, if you are writing to convince employees that their participation in a certain endeavor is needed, emphasize what is of value to your workforce. If overtime will be required, let them know it is a temporary situation and emphasize that it reflects positively on the company and hence on each person directly.

DEVELOPING THE "WRITE" STUFF

Managers who write sloppy, unclear, or convoluted correspondence and documents do themselves no career favors.

Consider a 2004 survey by the Business Roundtable and the National Commission on Writing for America's Families, Schools, and Colleges, which found that 51 percent of all companies surveyed take candidates' writing ability into account when considering them for a higher position. Moreover, the ability to write well could prove decisive when seeking a job. "People who cannot write and communicate clearly will not be hired and are unlikely to last long enough to be considered for promotion," according to the report.

The bottom line? If you are serious about advancing your managerial career, polish your writing skills.

SOURCE: "Writing: A Ticket to Work or a Ticket Out," College Board's National Commission on Writing (September 2004).

THE BOTTOM LINE

Let them know you sympathize, and offer some token of appreciation in return for their continued commitment.

If you are writing to customers, focus on how you or your product can help them meet their needs. Consider this letter:

Dear Mr. Chen,

Your name was provided by a colleague, Fred Smith. Fred suggested you might be interested in our digital pager, which will be unveiled at the Online Communication trade show in Chicago. If you are attending the show, I can make arrangements for you to get a trial version of the pager and determine if it meets the needs of your mobile workforce. Please let me know if I can help. Thank you for your time.

Sincerely,

John Doe
Marketing Manager

Although this letter does not guarantee a response, it offers Mr. Chen some compelling reasons to consider replying. First, the reference to someone he knows is a tip-off that it was sent by a credible source. Second, it spells out the reasons Mr. Chen might be interested in learning more about the product. It closes by offering him something special: a preview of the digital pager before it arrives on the market.

Striking the Right Tone

Whether you are writing to make a request or to persuade, remember that tremendous good will is generated by including three magic words: "please" and "thank you." Use these words as a regular practice, particularly in all your correspondence, whether you are the boss or a rank-and-file employee. Remember that even if you are sending out a mandate, it is wise to let it come across as a firm, polite request rather than an order.

Revising and Editing

Before sending any written message, reread it several times, looking for any errors. Double-check the spelling of unusual words. If you are writing an important business letter, consult with a colleague. Are you certain the person's name, title, and company are spelled correctly? Have you used your word-processing software to check your grammar, punctuation, and spelling? When in doubt, have you consulted a standard dictionary or grammar guide? Only after you complete these steps is your message ready for delivery.

DIGITAL
COMMUNICATION

> "There are managers so preoccupied with their e-mail messages that they never look up from their screens to see what's happening in the nondigital world."
>
> —Dr. Mihaly Csikszentmihalyi, author of *Flow* and *Creativity*

For most businesspeople, e-mail has become the most common form of written communication. Because many workers spend most of the day "wired" to computers, e-mail is the only way to reach them quickly and reliably.

In general, people use e-mail to quickly exchange time-sensitive information. E-mail is easy to use and removes the headache of printing out letters and stuffing envelopes. E-mail potentially enables managers to get more done in a single day than they would by chasing down the same information via phone or fax or waiting for letters to arrive in the mail.

Throughout the chapter, we will explore common forms of digital communication—especially e-mail—and examine when it is best to use them.

COMMUNICATING VIA E-MAIL

E-mail stands for electronic mail, but you don't need a wall outlet to be plugged in to work correspondence. In this wired world, your e-mail in-box no longer resides solely in your desktop computer, but instead travels wherever you, your laptop, or your handheld device go. E-mail is as likely to be crafted on a BlackBerry during a bumpy cab ride as on a laptop in a quiet home office. The ease with which people can reach others through e-mail has resulted in far more information being exchanged than in the era of typewritten letters. This volume has its advantages and disadvantages.

E-mail is the most pervasive and useful communication tool to emerge since the telephone. A 2006 survey by the staffing company Office Team found that 71 percent of executives use e-mail as their preferred method of communication, whereas only 27 percent were doing so in 2001. Employees in most businesses use e-mail internally to set up meetings, ask for information, and exchange opinions and ideas. Organizations use e-mail externally to share information with business partners, investors, or customers. E-mail enables companies to swap vital information with suppliers and vendors, and makes it possible for geographically dispersed employees to collaborate in ways never before possible. Both you and your staff have little choice but to learn to express yourself effectively via e-mail.

The **BIG** Picture

FUTURE PREDICTIONS

According to Bill Gates, founder of Microsoft, in the future, new technologies will make communication a multi-sensory experience of sight and sound. "Unified communications technologies will eliminate the barriers between the communications modes—e-mail, voice, web conferencing and more—that we use every day. They will enable us to close the gap between the devices we use to contact people when we need information and the applications and business processes where we use that information. The impact on productivity, creativity and collaboration will be profound," predicts Gates.

SOURCE: "The Unified Communications Revolution" by Bill Gates, Microsoft (June 26, 2006).

Self-Assessment Quiz

DOES YOUR E-MAIL MEASURE UP?

Read each of the following statements and indicate whether you agree or disagree. Then check your score at the end.

1. I always organize my thoughts before composing e-mail.

   ○ Agree   ○ Disagree

2. I make time to personalize each message.

   ○ Agree   ○ Disagree

3. I always type the recipient's e-mail address last.

   ○ Agree   ○ Disagree

4. I prepare thoughtful subject lines to elicit the best responses.

   ○ Agree   ○ Disagree

5. I make sure my message is concise and direct.

   ○ Agree   ○ Disagree

6. I pay strict attention to grammar, punctuation, and typos.

   ○ Agree   ○ Disagree

7. My intended audience is always foremost in my mind.

   ○ Agree   ○ Disagree

8. I commonly use "please" and "thank you" in my e-mail.

   ○ Agree   ○ Disagree

Scoring

Give yourself 1 point for every question you answered "Agree" and 0 points for every question you answered "Disagree."

Analysis

6–8	Consider yourself an authority on how to write business e-mail.
4–5	You need to brush up on e-mail practices and etiquette.
0–3	Consider taking a course in online business communications.

E-Mail Format

Although e-mail is used frequently as a casual form of communication, important messages, to be effective, should imitate the structure of a formal letter. Messages should consist of an introduction, a body of brief but meaningful information, and a conclusion. Treat the content of an e-mail with the same care you would other writing. Be scrupulous about grammar, punctuation, and language.

The recipient. Although the recipient field is at the very top of most e-mail formats—and thus, users typically type the recipient's e-mail address first—it should actually be the *last* thing you complete before sending your message. Get in the habit of typing recipients' e-mail addresses after you have thoroughly proofread your message, since it reduces the chances of your hitting "Send" prematurely—a common error that is stomach-churning if you haven't really completed editing your message for tone, grammar, and spelling. After you type in or select the recipient's e-mail address, double-check that it is correct. You don't want to send your message anonymously into cyberspace or to the wrong person. This could easily happen if your e-mail program stores addresses and automatically recognizes and fills in the addresses of recent e-mail recipients.

The subject line. Always include a pithy header or subject line to grab your reader's attention. Messages that arrive without an indication of their content or that fail to identify the sender are likely to be discarded as junk e-mail.

For relevance, correlate the topic of your e-mail to an item or event your readers will instantly recognize, such as conferences, previous phone calls, or other business events. If your company has been discussing meaningful policy changes with employees, for example, an e-mail with the subject line "Payday changes" is sure to get the needed response.

"Do not say a little in many words but a great deal in a few."

—Pythagoras,
Greek philosopher
(circa 582–507 BCE)

If you need a response quickly, say so in your subject line, as in "Program notes/Answers needed today." Because most e-mail programs truncate subject lines after 40 characters, make every word count. Remember that your subject lines will ultimately help you track what has been communicated on a certain topic.

The greeting. Whenever possible, address the recipient by name and with an appropriate salutation. Greetings such as "Dear Mr. Smith," "Esteemed Shareholders," "Loyal Customers," or "Valued Employees" are formal. An e-mail to someone you communicate with regularly— your manager, subordinate, or coworker—would not be treated with the same formality. In that case, a simple "Hi Mary and John" will do. Regardless of the recipient, however, courtesy

TAKE CARE WITH YOUR DISTRIBUTION

Many businesspeople are overwhelmed by the sheer number of e-mails they receive and have to respond to, sometimes as many as a few hundred a day! For that reason, you should be discriminating when deciding on the list of recipients for e-mails you send.

The "To" field should include only the names of principal recipients, those who are most likely to be affected or motivated to action after receiving your message.

The "cc" (the virtual carbon copy) should include people who need the information for background purposes. You might, for instance, send an e-mail to a departmental supervisor and "cc" the supervisor's assistant.

and professionalism should be your watchwords. Use a colon or comma to separate the greeting from the main body of text. Colons formerly were the norm, but commas are lighter and friendlier. A dash is even more casual and even breezy.

Body of message. Don't annoy readers by belaboring the point. Readers should know from the first few words of your e-mail exactly how this message affects them. Devote at least one paragraph, which in electronic communication

Plan B

The "bcc" (blind carbon copy) functions in the same way as the cc except that the names in this field are not seen by other recipients. Use this field sparingly, since it's arguably unfair to the recipient who is not fully aware of who else might be receiving the same message.

It is bad form and a breach of e-mail etiquette to use the "Reply to all" option indiscriminately, especially for messages of a sensitive nature. Also, if 15 people received the same e-mail you did, be mindful that not everyone wants to know your response, particularly if it is a one-word answer like "Sure."

may consist of no more than one or two brief sentences, to the main point of your message. A second paragraph might be necessary to reiterate or clarify your main points. Be clear about priorities or items that require immediate action. Conclude by offering phone numbers, e-mail addresses, or Web sites so readers can obtain additional information.

Finally, accuracy in language and grammar is paramount. Use the spell-check and grammar-check feature of your e-mail program to help you find and correct errors before you hit "Send." With these features at your fingertips, there is little excuse for errors cropping up in important business e-mail.

Note that e-mail messages are short and shorn of any unnecessary ornaments of speech. This is especially effective when communicating with someone who tends to travel and therefore reads e-mail on a cell phone or PDA. In such instances, sentences should not exceed a few words in a simple text message.

The signature. Conclude your message with an e-mail "signature" that includes your name, official title, company name, mailing address, phone and fax numbers, e-mail address, and perhaps a hyperlink to your company's web site. Not only does the signature provide a nice finish to your message, but combined with an appropriate greeting and carefully thought-out subject header, it goes a long way toward eliciting the desired response. In digital parlance, these three elements make up what is known as "Netiquette"—internet communications etiquette.

Applying this format enables you to convey information in a manner that bespeaks professionalism and accessibility. Here is an example:

To all at Smith Company:

Beginning July 4, 2008, payday will move to Friday from Wednesday. Your first check under the new system will include the appropriate adjustment. Please contact me at extension 3534 if you have questions. Thank you.

Marta Bauman
Payroll Specialist
Smith Company
299 Rutledge Street
Baxter, VT 05654
802/654-3534 direct
802/654-2600 fax
mbauman@smithco.us
www.smithco.us

E-Mails That Report or Inform

Companies use e-mail in various ways. Perhaps none has such immediate benefits as the ability to keep employees informed of rapidly changing developments in your company. Informational e-mail messages are a great method for disseminating information to a vast number of people. Human resources departments use e-mail to

CASE *FILE*

AVOID E-MAIL LAYOFFS

Employees who are being let go should find out the bad news from their managers. Seems sensible, right?

Yet Radio Shack Corp. took another approach when laying off around 400 people at its Fort Worth, Texas, headquarters in August 2006. The national electronics retailer used e-mail to notify workers that their jobs were being eliminated. Here is an excerpt from the e-mail sent to employees who were let go: "The work force reduction notification is currently in progress. Unfortunately your position is one that has been eliminated."

Radio Shack defended its method, saying workers knew in advance the e-mail notifications would be coming. "It was important to notify people as quickly as

inform employees of changes in company policies or to announce new developments within their companies. Customer service departments routinely send e-mail messages to update customers about product shipments or to resolve complaints. Companies with global operations increasingly rely on digital communications, including e-mail and instant messaging software, to help far-flung employees collaborate on team-based projects.

possible," a Radio Shack spokeswoman told the *Dallas Morning News.* "They had 30 minutes to collect their thoughts, make phone calls, and say goodbye to employees before they went to meet with senior leaders."

Radio Shack's electronic pink slips, however, earned the company much negative publicity. It seems that while Radio Shack indeed conducted layoffs "as quickly as possible," it also demonstrated that e-mail is not always the most effective—or professional—business tool to communicate information to employees.

SOURCE: "Radio Shack Lays Off 403 via E-mail" by Ieva M. Augstums and Maria Halkia, *Dallas Morning News* (August 31, 2006); "'You've Got Mail: You're Fired,'" *The Oregonian* (September 1, 2006).

When supplying information in an e-mail, get right to the point. Keep your sentences short and your message brief.

If the information you are sharing is complex, divide the text into sections and use subheads to highlight the subject of each section.

If the recipients are all colleagues, you can adopt a less formal tone than if the e-mail were addressed to people outside the company. For instance, you might write:

Hi everyone,

Our engineers are reviewing drawings for the new building. They tell me they'll have working drawings ready on Friday. I will bring them to the status meeting and hand-deliver copies to each of you. Please let me know if you have questions.

Thanks,
John

For messages intended for people you don't know well, especially those outside your company, keep the tone more formal, use recipients' titles, and spell out the names of specific projects. In the e-mail above, for example, "drawings for the new building" might become "drawings for the Millenial Aerospace Design Center."

Instead of referring simply to a status meeting, you might offer specific information: "I will bring them to our status meeting at 2 PM on Thursday, June 10, in our offices in Chicago. Please let me know if you would like to join us." Finally, you would sign off with your full name and title.

E-Mails That Request or Persuade

When sending e-mail to request information from another person, the degree of formality depends on two things: how well you know the person, and the level of serious discussion required. A simple request such as asking for directions to

Behind the Numbers

COMMUNICATION AND LEADERSHIP

Although 40 percent of managers and executives exhibit characteristics that are associated with strong leadership, about one-third lack the skills required to manage people effectively, according to a survey by Right Management Consultants. Communication skills top the list of traits that employees consider desirable in managers. The survey findings were based on responses of human resource managers from 133 organizations.

The most highly desired skills that companies seek when hiring managers are listed below in descending order of importance:

Good communication skills	47%
Sense of vision	44%
Honesty	32%
Decisiveness	31%
Favorable relationships with workforce	26%
Intelligence	23%
Creativity	22%
Attention to detail	21%

SOURCE: "Thirty Percent of Managers and Executives Lack Necessary Management Skills," Right Management Consultants (September 21, 2004).

a customer's place of business demands a more casual tone than an e-mail intended to formally recruit local business to participate in a chamber of commerce charity event.

Some requests need to be persuasive. The goal is to get recipients to acknowledge your message, even if they aren't willing to make a commitment initially. If you need someone's cooperation to get a project off the ground, make your wishes

Dos & Don'ts ☑

DEVELOPING GOOD E-MAIL HABITS

Although e-mail is faster and more immediate than most other forms of written communication, don't make the mistake of hastily composing messages that can misconstrue your intentions, meaning, or facts. Be sure to practice these essential e-mail habits.

☐ Do keep your messages brief and make each word count.

☐ Do clearly identify the topic in the subject line.

☐ Do address recipients by name.

☐ Don't discuss sensitive or proprietary information.

☐ Don't discuss personnel matters with individual employees in e-mail.

known immediately, and outline the benefits of the undertaking for the other person. Spell out in the subject line the nature of your request. A journalist seeking information could let prospective sources know her intentions by writing, "Urgent media request/Story on workers' attitudes/Your input requested" in the subject line. That way it won't take the recipient too much time to figure out the contents of the e-mail.

- ☐ Don't send unsolicited e-mail to customers.
- ☐ Do request people's participation with courtesy.
- ☐ Don't hit "Reply to all" unless you know everyone needs to read your message.
- ☐ Don't include defamatory or threatening language.
- ☐ Do check spelling, punctuation, grammar.
- ☐ Do reread your message before sending.
- ☐ Do type e-mail addresses last and check that they are correctly spelled before sending.

E-Mails That Respond

While e-mails that inform tend to impart new information, those that respond to another person's message address topics in an ongoing conversation. When responding to any e-mail, include or attach a portion of the original message (or "e-mail thread" if several messages have been exchanged). Most e-mail programs offer a "Reply" option that automatically appends the message to which you are replying. If this option is not available, you don't need to include all the

CASE FILE

E-MAIL GONE HAYWIRE

Corporate e-mail that is privately exchanged can easily become public knowledge. Hewlett-Packard even found itself in hot water with federal investigators after corporate e-mail messages exposed the company's efforts to gain private phone records of its board of directors, as well as of employees and journalists, in an attempt to plug boardroom leaks of privileged company information.

The e-mail exchanges were exposed by media outlets, and the explosive story shook the business community. HP chairman of the board Patricia Dunn was forced to resign and charged with felonies, along with five others. The resulting original message, but just enough to provide context for your response. This is particularly important when you resume a conversation after a long delay. Include the original message thread in your response so both of you can pick up where you left off.

Responding to e-mails in a timely fashion is not only good manners—it could be critical to the success of your job or business. For example, if a customer has a complaint about defective merchandise, or simply wants to know where to purchase an item, failing to reply quickly could harm your customer-service reputation.

fallout spawned congressional inquiries, inflamed investors, and left HP with a black eye.

The HP episode serves as an object lesson for managers on how *not* to use e-mail. Even as the company tries to shake off the scandal, the e-mail messages are being circulated widely around the internet. The messages will last forever—giving HP and its managerial crew a painful reminder of the dangers of careless e-mail use.

SOURCE: "H.P. Investigators Sought Meeting with Top Leaders" by Matt Richtel, *New York Times* (September 21, 2006); "Five Are Charged in HP Scandal" by Clint Swett, *Sacramento Bee* (October 5, 2006).

E-Mail Etiquette

There are some basic ground rules to observe for business e-mail. Above all, be courteous. Remember that the recipient of your message is probably extremely busy. Be respectful, but don't sound cloying. Put simply, show consideration for the person receiving the message.

If you are writing as a representative of your firm, especially to someone you don't know, it's best to err on the side of a more formal tone. This includes spelling out words and limiting your use of abbreviations.

Although you should aim for precision in all your communications, language is often clipped, capitalization is sometimes neglected, and abbreviations may pop up in informal e-mails. For example, many e-mail users dispense with capitalization in e-mails to recipients they know well, since writing in lowercase is much faster and easier—especially when using a handheld device such as a Treo or a BlackBerry.

Internet shorthand—using acronyms or abbreviations for common phrases, such as "TNT" for "till next time," "TTYL" for "talk to you later," or "SYS" for "see you soon"—is increasingly finding its way into e-mail business communication. But this abbreviated form of writing may be too casual and even playful for some work environments, so make sure that Internet shorthand is accepted in your organization before you use it.

Use abbreviations or acronyms only in your e-mail exchanges with coworkers or others who understand the lingo, and be sure you know what the terms you use stand for. Some might be a substitute for profane language, and some recipients may find them offensive.

Dos & Don'ts ☑

THE ART OF E-MAIL ETIQUETTE

Set an example for your employees and peers by practicing good e-mail etiquette (or "netiquette").

☐ Do reply promptly to e-mails.

☐ Do be polite, but not verbose— make your point quickly.

☐ Don't respond to chain letters.

☐ Don't type in capital letters. It's the e-mail equivalent of SHOUTING.

☐ Don't include too many hyperlinks or elaborate formatting.

☐ Do be selective when sending replies to all recipients.

☐ Do use the blind carbon copy (bcc) function for an e-mail with a large distribution list to avoid publishing all the recipients' addresses.

☐ Do close with an e-mail signature.

☐ Do not respond to a recipient in an e-mail on which you've been blind-copied.

When responding to several people at once, be careful about using the "Reply to all" option and inadvertently passing on other people's e-mail addresses. Few things do worse damage to your business reputation than being careless with someone's personal information.

Finally, don't send a time-sensitive e-mail too late in the business day for people to respond to it, or so that you can put off discussing an important matter. Also, avoid sending messages when you know recipients may not have access to their accounts or will be unable to respond in a timely fashion. Your e-mail is going to be received in a much better spirit if it doesn't seem strategically timed to the person's disadvantage.

The Shortcomings of E-Mail

Because it is easy to use and it relays messages instantly, e-mail is one of the most efficient business communication tools. But it is not ideal for every situation. Discussing sensitive or privileged information with employees or outsiders, for instance, is best handled in person. Likewise, it's preferable to take an employee aside when discussing a matter that has a direct personal bearing on that individual, rather than risk inadvertently revealing personal information by sending e-mail across unsecured computer networks.

One of the biggest dangers of e-mail is that some people use it to evade direct communication with other workers, especially when the subject is unpleasant or controversial. In many cases, e-mail is a poor substitute for face-to-face interaction. It does not convey the nuances of

WORK **FLOW** TOOLS

COPING WITH E-MAIL DELUGE

Designate a specific time each day to respond to e-mail.

Scan messages first, read them thoroughly later.

Respond promptly to the most urgent messages.

Delete any junk mail and spam—unsolicited messages from unknown senders—that is not automatically filtered by your e-mail system.

Keep your outgoing messages brief.

Delete or file the e-mails you have already responded to or dealt with.

CASE *FILE*

BANNING E-MAIL FOR A DAY

PBD Worldwide Fulfillment Services took an unusual step to prevent e-mail from replacing face time with coworkers. On Fridays, PBD's employees are permitted to exchange e-mail with customers and others outside the office—but not with internal colleagues.

"One of the values of our company is to work better as a team, and teamwork does not work real well when all you do is e-mail each other," CEO Scott A. Dockter said on NPR's "All Things Considered."

The policy seems to be working. According to Dockter it has helped PBD significantly cut e-mail traffic inside the company. Such efforts should be commended. They result in an increase in personal interaction between coworkers and thus promote a tighter-knit corporate culture.

SOURCE: "E-mail Takes a Holiday, at Least for One Day" by Melissa Block, National Public Radio's "All Things Considered" (September 29, 2006).

emotion, pick up inflection and tone of voice, or, of course, capture facial expressions.

Many business situations merit sitting down with another person to resolve an issue.

Managers, in particular, need to anticipate how others might respond to their news or messages, before deciding the best way to communicate them. Before sending an e-mail, always ask yourself: Will I benefit from seeing how the recipient reacts to my news or message? Will the recipient's response be more productive if she receives the news personally?

Finally, one of the shortcomings of e-mail is the technology itself. E-mails get lost in cyberspace. Stored messages can be permanently destroyed by a computer crash. Whenever you send an important e-mail message that you suspect has not reached its intended recipient, follow up with a phone call. Also consider printing a backup hard copy of critical messages for your records or files.

Create an E-Mail Policy—and Enforce It

As a manager, part of your responsibility may be to help establish policies governing the appropriate uses of e-mail for your department, division, company, or organization. Employees are less likely to abuse the privilege of using your company's e-mail system if they have been given clear guidelines.

Whenever possible, consult with your legal department or counsel when establishing e-mail guidelines. Standard e-mail policies, however, generally stipulate that e-mail should be used only for company business. Sending or storing e-mails containing pornographic material, off-color jokes, inappropriate remarks, or e-mails characterized by vulgar or profane language or by remarks that

Dos & Don'ts ☑

PERSONAL E-MAIL AT WORK

Business e-mail is a powerful tool, but like other tools, it can cause damage if not used correctly. Following a few simple rules can protect privacy and prevent embarrassment, wrecked careers, and worse.

☐ Do know your company's policy on e-mail.

☐ Don't send personal e-mail, including e-mail jokes, video files, photos, or other non-work-related material, from your work e-mail account.

☐ Do tell colleagues and friends not to send non-work-related material to your work e-mail account.

☐ Don't send large files, such as photos of your lake house or digital videos of your nephews, without first informing recipients. Large files can clog in-boxes.

☐ Do find out if your e-mail messages are being screened and read by your superiors.

might be interpreted as tacitly condoning sexual harassment or discrimination based on sex, race, or religion should be strictly forbidden.

Make it clear that the company owns any e-mail that is sent or stored in its computers and that management has the right to access, view, and monitor employees' e-mails. In order to enforce e-mail policies, consider purchasing filtering software and other technologies to help you monitor how employees are using your

Behind the Numbers

CONDUCTING PERSONAL BUSINESS?

According to a 2005 survey on e-mail user behavior conducted by consulting firms Mirapoint and Radicati Group, a significant portion of corporate e-mail sent and received is not work-related:

72% of respondents forwarded personal e-mails from their corporate accounts.

12% shared music files through work e-mail.

97% had a personal e-mail account.

62% sent work-related e-mails from their personal accounts.

SOURCE: "Nearly 25 Percent of Corporate Email Is Personal in Nature," *CRM Today* (November 23, 2005).

CASE *FILE*

E-MAIL AND REGULATORY COMPLIANCE

Managers are learning that what they say in an e-mail can come back to haunt them. The widely publicized corporate scandal at Enron Corp. exposed the liability corporations and their managers may face because of ill-advised e-mail.

The federal government's prosecution of Enron executives on fraud and other charges involved publicly posting nearly two million of the energy firm's e-mails on the Internet. These included messages that were highly embarrassing at best and at worst incriminating.

Managers with publicly traded companies—or that do business with such organizations—should be aware that the e-mail messages they send may come under the scrutiny of regulators. It is impossible to anticipate this scenario, which is why it pays to communicate honestly and transparently. The convicted Enron executives undoubtedly never thought their e-mail discussing illicit accounting schemes would be publicly known.

SOURCE: "Science Puts Enron E-Mail to Use" by Ryan Singel, *Wired* (January 30, 2006).

e-mail system, including reading the messages being sent.

IM: SENDING MESSAGES IN AN INSTANT

E-mail isn't the only form of electronic communication being used by companies. Many organizations use "Instant Messaging" (IM) programs, which allow one person to send text messages to other people in real time.

Senders know whether the person they want to communicate with is online and readily available to "chat." Thus, IM is an even faster form of online communication than e-mail, since both the sender and receiver of a message are able to respond to each other within seconds.

A growing number of organizations are taking a shine to IM communications, attracted by its immediacy and low cost of implementation. Research firm IDC reports that 70 percent of companies have employees that rely heavily on instant messaging to transact vital business. For work teams that need to collaborate across geographic boundaries, IM technology is a particularly useful communication tool for getting work done.

When communicating via IM, users frequently adopt Internet shorthand or commonly used abbreviations and acronyms that have gained acceptance by users. Because IM thrives on a more casual tone, it is normally used for internal communications only, rather than for sharing information with business contacts outside the company. Finally, in some systems you must know the recipient's "screen name"

Dos & Don'ts ☑

INSTANT COMMUNICATION

Analysts predict instant messaging could soon supplant e-mail as the preferred method of corporate communication. But managers should use IM tools wisely.

☐ Do use IM for one-to-one chats with coworkers.

☐ Don't use IM to send proprietary or confidential data.

☐ Don't conduct personal messaging while at work.

☐ Don't mouth off—like e-mail, instant messages can be archived or accessed by others.

☐ Do adhere to your company's policy governing IM use.

to communicate via IM. A screen name is the online "handle" by which people identify themselves anonymously to other users.

PDAs (Personal Digital Assistants)

Some Internet-based e-mail programs allow users to access their e-mails remotely, via laptops, a home computer, some cellular phones, and wireless personal digital assistants (PDAs). In fact, in today's fast-paced business environment, wireless PDAs or handheld devices, such as the Treo and the BlackBerry, have become popular business tools, since they allow people to stay connected through e-mail regardless of where they are.

Because the keypads on wireless devices are small and not as practical, users limit their responses to brief messages—sometimes one-word answers—and avoid using capital letters or even punctuation. Messages sent from wireless devices should always include an automatic signature or notification that the message was sent on such a device so that recipients know the user's limitations and won't expect the same formality.

Precision
On Paper

"If a leader can't get a message across clearly and motivate others to act on it, then having a message doesn't even matter."

—Gilbert Amelio,
former CEO of National Semiconductor
and Apple Computer

As pervasive as electronic writing has become, more traditional forms of communication are still alive and well. No business manager can advance far without knowing how to write formal letters, reports, and other longer pieces of official correspondence.

Internal memos still get circulated within the walls of companies. Letters that give thanks, praise, or critique should flow easily from your pen (or keyboard), since you will be called on often to produce them. In addition, you must learn to present cogent arguments in memos or lengthier business reports, which are still widely used.

All of these more "traditional" forms of writing package broad concepts into easily digestible pieces. They are not as immediate as electronic communication. In fact, they are designed to force readers to linger over the information, soaking up its details.

Being conversant with e-mail, with its lax rules and casual tone, will not help you in formal writing, where accuracy is paramount and poor language skills can torpedo the brightest business proposal. Your ability to deftly handle a range of writing tasks may spell the difference between advancing in your career or getting stuck in a rut.

CRAFTING SMART, SNAPPY MEMOS

"Did you get the memo?" Internal memorandums, or memos, are among the most common forms of business communication. Memos are brief documents used to impart information between a select group of people within (or associated with) the same company. Memos are typically short—sometimes they don't exceed one page in length, although they often stretch to two or more pages if highly complex or technical information is being presented. As a manager, you may be called on to draft memos regarding any number of things—from announcing a direct report's promotion, to reminding employees of important dates, to presenting items of more substantial import. For that reason, the ability to craft memos that both get attention and elicit the desired response is a vital managerial skill.

Create memos on a standard piece of paper ($8\frac{1}{2}$ inches by 11 inches). Leave 1-inch margins at the top and bottom of each page and 1 inch to $1\frac{1}{4}$ inches for both left and right margins. Memos consist of two main components: a heading and the body of information to be presented.

Heading. The heading lists the following information: the names of recipients, the name of the sender, the date the memo is being circulated, and a subject line briefly describing the contents. Use double spacing to separate the four components of the heading. Memos are instantly recognizable due to this format, an example of which is below:

To:

From:

Date:

Subject:

Known as the vertical format, this is the structure commonly used by most companies.

Another option is a horizontal format, which organizes the elements in elongated fashion across a page. Note that each item is double-spaced.

To: Date:

From: Subject:

Choice of structure is largely a matter of corporate preference. Regardless of which format you use, remember that every memo needs to contain the four elements in the heading, as listed above.

Use the "To" field to list the names of all the people to whom the memo is being sent. (Make sure to add a "cc" field to list the names of people who will receive a copy of the memo.) If the memo is to coworkers, it is probably not necessary to address each person by his or her job title. Simply including their full names in a basic distribution list will suffice.

However, if you are addressing superiors, include their titles and be sure to address the recipient formally. Always err on the side of formality in a memo, even if you know the person well. For example, never address a colleague by his or her nickname.

Always double-check the spelling of recipients' names. If you are unsure of the spelling, consult a company directory. Few things offend people more than seeing their names misspelled, particularly by someone who ought to know how to spell them correctly.

In the "From" field, fully spell out your name and handwrite your initials next to it. If your memo is intended for employees with whom you are familiar or have an established working relationship, then your title won't be necessary. Managers in large organizations, however, sometimes have to draft memos addressed to people of higher rank whom they have not met or know only slightly. In such instances, include your full

The **BIG** Picture

FAILURE TO COMMUNICATE

Managers who express themselves clearly in writing stand a better chance of succeeding and of helping their organizations thrive. Writing also enhances verbal communication skills. On the other hand, poor communication with employees results in:

- Lost revenue opportunities

- Drops in productivity

- Decline in employee morale

- Increased job stress

- Dissatisfied customers

- Inability to make informed decisions

- High employee turnover

Dos & Don'ts ☑

MEMO CHECKLIST

Effective memo writing is an acquired skill. Until you have mastered the form, it pays to double-check your finished product to make sure you haven't overlooked basic elements. One simple omission can detract from an otherwise well-crafted message.

☐ Do follow your company's preferred memo format.

☐ Don't forget the four elements of the heading: To, From, Date, Subject.

☐ Don't forget to double-space subheadings.

☐ Don't address people by their nicknames in the heading.

☐ Do include job titles for people of higher rank.

☐ Do clearly state the purpose of your memo.

☐ Do summarize previous discussions.

☐ Do provide subheads to help readers scan relevant content.

☐ Do use bullet points and headers to break up longer memos.

name and official job title, separated by a comma or placed on the line below.

Spell out the specific date the memo is distributed. Finally, your subject line should complete the header by providing a synopsis of the detailed information contained in the memo. This tagline should serve as a preview of what people should expect to read.

To: John Cox, Mary Wilson, and Debby Branigan

Cc: Dan Howard, Chief Financial Officer

From: Steve McIntyre *SM*
          Director of Accounts Payable

Date: June 6, 2003

Subject: Implementing software upgrades for
          accounts payable system

Content. Memos are not intended to be exhaustive. Their purpose is to sum up key information. The person reading it should know at a glance whether the information you are presenting is urgent or can be deferred for later action.

Don't use ornate speech or load the memo with jargon. In fact, you should shun acronyms and abbreviations unless they are technical or scientific and will be easily recognized by your audience. Aim for clarity and simplicity.

Dos & Don'ts ☑

AVOIDING MEMO MISTAKES

How a memo is written is as important as the information it contains.

☐ Do use a cordial tone.

☐ Don't use ornate language. Good memos convey key points at a glance.

☐ Do present important information right away, in logical order.

☐ Do outline the steps you plan to take or action you recommend.

☐ Don't forget to include attachments if you intend to use them.

☐ Don't present too much information at once.

☐ Do guide readers to the most salient points.

☐ Don't fail to provide needed background or context.

☐ Don't overuse superfluous clauses ("In order to," "Due to," "Because of," etc.).

Don't let casual or careless language creep into memos, because they could be saved, circulated around the company, or even wind up in

CASE *FILE*

THE POWER OF THE PEN

The greatest business leaders have always known the power of communicating by writing. Jack Welch, former CEO of General Electric, was in the habit of sending handwritten notes to workers at all levels within the company. Some employees reportedly even framed the gregarious Welch's letters as mementos of his appreciation. Likewise Berkshire Hathaway CEO Warren Buffett pens an annual corporate memo that is eagerly anticipated by analysts, shareholders, and the company's employees.

SOURCE: "Making Yourself Understood" by Des Dearlove and Stuart Crainer, *Across the Board* (May/June 2004).

the hands of people outside your organization. Sound cordial and accessible without sacrificing professionalism.

Begin your memo by stating its objective in a strong opening sentence. Writing experts sometimes call this a "purpose statement." It should encapsulate your reason for writing the memo in the first place. Try to answer as many of the "five Ws" as possible: who, what, when, where, and why.

Supporting or clarifying information should follow the purpose statement in a succeeding paragraph. Provide enough information for people to make a decision or take specified action. Lay out the details of what is to happen next. If possible, specify the action you plan to take.

In the closing paragraph reemphasize the main subject of your memo and encourage readers to contact you. If you are sending other documents with your memo, be sure to mention them.

Below is an example of a typical memo:

To: Joe Smith, Carla Sanchez

From: Bonnie Smith *BS*
         First Aid Training Team Leader

Date: June 6, 2006

Subject: First Aid Training Schedule

We have set a tentative schedule with the Red Cross to provide onsite training to all members serving on the first aid team.

The Red Cross staff will come to our office next Wednesday, June 3, and Thursday, June 4, to provide training in basic first aid and CPR. We would like to train daytime and nightshift employees together in sessions from 6 p.m. to 8 p.m. All employees will receive overtime pay for attending these sessions. I will meet separately with the day and nightshift associates to ensure all employees are scheduled to attend one of these two sessions.

I am also attaching advance copies of the training materials. Thank you for volunteering to serve on our first aid team. This is a very important contribution to the safety and health of all our employees and will help us maintain compliance with OSHA and company regulations.

Note several things about this memo. First, the author assumes those reading it already know something about the subject: first aid. Second, it opens with information that will interest the readers: the schedule has been finalized. It then offers details about the schedule.

Method. Memos are generally written in two main formats: Deductive and inductive. Deductive memos present information in descending order of importance. This is useful for readers who share common knowledge about a subject. Deductive memos present information in logical order, as opposed to chronological order. Your most critical point should be stated first, followed by supporting information in successive paragraphs.

Inductive memos, on the other hand, place ideas in increasing order of importance. Induction is useful when managers need to break bad news. It enables you to logically state the reasons that have led to the conclusion that the reader is about to draw. Background is given first, followed by any supporting data. Presenting this data first enables you to build momentum toward the most salient issue.

THE ENDURING LETTER

Despite the prevalence of e-mail in the work-place, people continue to rely on formal business letters as an effective form of communication. The continued use of letters underscores how important it is for aspiring managers of the "wired generation" to master this form of writing. A good letter expresses ideas in as few words, and as clearly as possible.

Red Flags ✕◆

PHRASES TO AVOID

Many business letters fail to achieve their goals because their authors use stilted, cliched, or meaningless phrases, terms, and jargon. Steer clear of these phrases, which are often the mark of bad business writing:

* **To be perfectly honest** – This has an insincere ring and suggests that previous discussions were somehow dishonest.

* **Needless to say** – So why bring it up?

* **Enclosed herewith** – Unless you're a lawyer, drop the officious tone of formality. A better alternative would be: "I've included a copy of the material with this letter."

Almost every letter is formal in nature, even when addressed to a business associate you may have known for years, since you never can be certain whose eyes may gaze upon your letter once it leaves the recipient's hands.

Letters communicate problems, solutions, ideas, plans, and suggestions. Managers write letters to existing customers to persuade them to buy a new product. A manager may target letters at former

- **As you know/as you are aware** – No need to state the obvious.

- **I am writing to inform you** – Instead of telling someone you are about to give him information, just present the information.

- **Please be advised** – You are about to provide advice anyway. So do it.

- **At your earliest convenience/as soon as possible** – Always specify a desired date or deadline for action. Their "earliest" convenience may be never.

SOURCE: "Don't Use These Phrases!" *Winning Strategies for Corporate Communication* (Communication Concepts, 1991).

customers in an attempt to win them back. Managers use letters to resolve complaints or request information. Sometimes they write letters of commendation to outstanding employees, while at other times letters of reprimand must be issued to employees not toeing the mark.

The purposes and uses of letters are too numerous to mention but generally fall into four broad categories: to notify, request, respond, and persuade.

Strive for Perfection

No writing medium demands as much discipline from managers as the business letter. Here, no room for error should be allowed. Recall the old adage: "You never get a second chance to make a first impression." Concentrate on making your initial impression a favorable one.

Letter Structure

Business letters share several particular features. These include: the date, the sender's address, the recipient's name and address, a greeting, a body of text, and a respectful closing.

Always use your company's official stationery or a standard 8½-by-11-inch paper. Set your right and left margins at 1 inch or 1¼ inches. Type the date, always spelling out the month (e.g., September 1, 2007). If you do not have company stationery, include your name and the company's address at the top of the page.

Skip one space between the date or address and write the name of the recipient next. If you don't know the recipient's name, make an effort

• POWER POINTS •

BEFORE YOU WRITE A LETTER

Sometimes it may not be obvious whether a letter is the best way to communicate. Before you write and mail a letter, ask yourself the following questions:

- Does the reader know me?

- Would a personal contact be more appropriate?

- What do I want this letter to accomplish?

- What questions do I need to ask?

- What would I like the reader to do for me?

- Have I suggested a course of action?

- Have I given the person enough background?

- How would I feel if this letter were addressed to me?

to find out. If you know the gender of the recipient, it is customary to include a courtesy title (Mr. Clark Johnson; Mrs. Joan Dole). Note that "Miss" is seldom used anymore. Most women in business today prefer "Ms."

List the official address of the recipient using the format established by the U.S. Postal Service. Include the official company name beneath the recipient's name (and if appropriate, his or her job title). Two other lines should immediately follow: one for the street address, and a separate line denoting locality, state, and zip code.

Greeting. Starting with "Dear" to open your letter is still the best approach ("Dear Mr. Clark"). If you do not know the gender of the recipient you can take the safe route and include the individual's first and last name ("Dear Chris Smith"). Other options include starting with the person's first name, but you'll run the risk of coming across as too informal. Other neutral-sounding openings, such as "Greetings," also may appear too flip or glib. If the letter is targeted to someone you have never met or know only as an acquaintance, keep it formal.

Formerly, people used the familiar "To whom it may concern" salutation when writing to a company rather than to a specific person within a company. This is no longer recommended. It sends the message that you weren't interested enough to take the time to find out who would be the most appropriate recipient. If you are not able to find out the appropriate person's name, opt for a generic greeting such as "Dear Customer Service Representative." Follow the greeting with a comma or, to be more formal, a colon.

Although form letters—letters written from a template, rather than drafted for a particular recipient—enable you to reach larger numbers of people more efficiently, their effectiveness is questionable. Because they appear so generic, many recipients toss them aside as junk mail. Although time-consuming, it may pay to personalize each letter you send.

Body of letter. Commit to making your point crystal clear from the outset. The worst reaction your letter can receive from a reader is: "So what?" Start by declaring your reason for writing. Write in a friendly and conversational tone, making sure to align your interests and needs with those of the reader. For example, if your reader buys hand tools and hand tools are what you sell, you might point out that industry forecasts predict a shortage of hand tools on the market within five years.

• POWER POINTS •

TARGETING YOUR PURPOSE

Business letters aim to accomplish several key objectives:

- Market, sell, or promote new products

- Clarify or provide information

- Reply to a person's request

- Give praise

- Convey good or bad news

Regardless of the message, make your introductory paragraph a grabber that compels the person to keep reading.

The remainder of your letter should buttress your main point. Follow your lead paragraph with details of the key points of your message.

> "There's so much riding on a business letter. A good friend might forgive misspelled words or poor grammar or even lapses in logic, but a business client probably won't be that forgiving."
>
> —Dr. Melvin J. Luthy,
> chief editor of WriteExpress

Use a minimum of words, but make sure they are well chosen. Make sentences brief but pack them with meaning. Sharpen and resharpen your sentences. Use as many paragraphs as needed, but keep each paragraph to about four or five lines. Be friendly without condescending to your reader. Use the pronouns "you" or "yours" and "I" to build a sense of familiarity. When writing to a coworker, adopt a collegial tone that lets the person know you consider her an equal.

Your final paragraph should serve as a summary and might even request the reader to take some action—for example, buy your hand tools at special prices and avoid being hit by the looming shortage. Always thank the recipient for considering your letter.

The closing. "Sincerely" preceding the signature is still widely used. Avoid "Sincerely yours," which readers may find stilted and insincere. Other acceptable closings include "Kind regards," "Best wishes," and "Respectfully" (though this last one is probably better suited for letters of complaint). The closing will be determined by the level of formality of the letter, how well you know your recipient, and the seriousness of your message.

Leave four spaces between the closing and your typed name. This space should be used for your handwritten signature. If you are enclosing materials with the letter, you should refer to them in the body of the letter and also include an "enclosure notation" at the end of the letter (e.g., "Encl: Spring catalog").

Conscientious writers take one final precaution before depositing a letter in the mailbox: They double-check the spelling of names and addresses on the envelope. Don't let elementary mistakes like a misspelled company name undermine a persuasive letter.

• POWER POINTS •

REMEMBER THE THREE P'S

Letter writers can benefit from a three-word mantra:

- Purpose

- Personalize

- Proofread

Formatting the Letter

Business letters are generally drafted in two common formats: Block text and modified block text. Most business letters embrace the block format, in which the entire letter is left-justified—meaning every line, including dates and closings, is set directly against the left margin—with a line space separating paragraphs. Many companies prefer to use the letter templates that are provided with computer software, such as Microsoft's Letter Wizard. If you use these templates, make sure the typeface and text alignment work well with your company's letterhead.

Choose a typeface, or font, that is visually appealing and in keeping with the degree of formality of your letter. The standard business font is Times Roman, using a point size of 11 or 12. Increasingly, though, other fonts are appearing in business writing, including Arial, Verdana, and Tahoma. Find out if your company has a preferred style.

Take a look at the sample letter below, which illustrates how to structure and format a strong business letter:

Jones Jordan Architects
5575 West 30 North Street
Salt Lake City, Utah 84101

September 1, 2007

Mr. James Adipietro
Ebersole Bauman Engineering, Inc.
1459 West Hudson Road, Suite B-100
Salt Lake City, Utah 84106

Dear Mr. Adipietro:

Mariel Bennett, a partner here at Jones Jordan, suggested I contact you. Our firm specializes in projects for educational institutions, including university research institutions and elementary and secondary schools. I am responsible for new-business initiatives.

Mariel mentioned that you met at the recent American Institute of Architects conference in Chicago. I understand you wanted more information about our firm and our project portfolio, which I am enclosing. After you have reviewed it, please let me know when would be a good time to meet to discuss a possible collaboration.

Thank you for your interest in our firm. Please do not hesitate to contact me at 801-669-7431 or james.jones@jjarchitects.com.

Sincerely,

James Jones

James Jones
Director of Marketing

Encl: Jones Jordan Architects portfolio

This letter aims to initiate a collaboration between two firms. Information is personalized, so that the letter does not seem like a form letter. An introduction and statement of purpose precede a brief paragraph of relevant information, followed by a closing paragraph that sums up the purpose of the letter and invites action. The tone is cordial and professional.

Pitch Letters

Pitch letters are the ultimate form of persuasive writing. The key to writing an effective pitch letter is to address not only your company's strengths, but also the particular needs of the company or individual you are pitching. This is true whether you are selling products, vying to land a new contract, or arranging business proposals that require cooperation from multiple stakeholders.

• POWER POINTS •

THE STRUCTURE OF A PITCH LETTER

To be truly effective, your pitch letter should:

- Lead with your proposal or recommendation.

- Spell out potential benefits if your recommendation is followed.

- Provide a deadline for action.

- Conclude by thanking the recipient for considering your proposal or recommendation.

Always make the item or idea you are pitching the focus of your lead sentence. After introducing your proposal, persuade readers with facts. Spell out any timetables for action, such as a deadline to either accept or reject your offer. Explain how the action you recommend will benefit the recipient.

You can't persuade the entire world to respond positively to your pitch. However, polished prose improves your chances of swaying people. Simplify your approach. Avoid passive sentences, which take the steam out of a powerful message. For example, don't talk about "service delivery"—write that you'll take care of the customer. Don't write that you are offering "solutions" if what you really sell is software.

Plan

BY ANY MEANS NECESSARY

If your pitch letters don't generate responses, follow up with a phone call or e-mail. You may find that the recipient of the letter values personal contact when considering a pitch. This doesn't mean a well-written letter is wasted. If the individual's interest is piqued by your call or e-mail, he or she is likely to refer back to your original letter.

Anticipate any questions or objections readers might have and try to answer them in the body of your letter. To the extent possible, short-circuit these objections by acknowledging they exist. Use candor to guide readers to the conclusion that any drawbacks are outweighed by the advantages of your product, service, or proposal.

Once you've finished writing the letter, read it aloud several times to yourself. Does the message flow? Have you repeated information? Ask someone you trust to read the letter as well and give you feedback. If they don't understand your meaning or find your letter persuasive, there is a good chance others won't either.

Cover Letter

An explanatory letter that accompanies a document is referred to as a "cover letter." Cover letters should accompany any package of materials that you send to someone (brochures, business proposals, sample products, etc.).

Cover letters should be addressed to a specific person, never to the generic "To whom it may concern." They should be short and sweet and should refer to the materials that they accompany. For example:

Dear Jeff,

It was nice seeing you at the trade show yesterday. Here is the information you wanted on our new solar-powered industrial drills, as well as results from our latest research on our newest model.

We are hoping to begin limited field testing of the drill sometime this fall, and several large industrial customers are on board already. I hope you find the research materials interesting.

I will be traveling during the next two weeks, but my assistant, Jason Wood, will be able to field questions in my absence. If you would like to discuss this further, Jason can schedule a time for us to meet. His direct line is 770-535-5767.

Sincerely,

Perry Preston

Perry Preston

Encl: SP-100 Drill Research

Dos & Don'ts ☑

ARE YOUR LETTERS EFFECTIVE?

If you sense your message isn't getting through, you may be inadvertently throwing up barriers to communication.

☐ Do use interesting language or examples to grab the reader's attention.

☐ Do respect others' time—sharp letters make memorable points quickly.

☐ Don't use language that could be misconstrued as offensive.

☐ Don't needlessly repeat information.

☐ Do thank the recipients of the letter for their time.

Thank-You Letter

Don't forget to write the all-important thank-you note to people who have helped you. Saying thank you is best done in a brief note. Given the volume of e-mail people receive, a thank-you received in the mail will make your message stand out. Although some people prefer to send handwritten notes, it is best to stick with a typed letter on company letterhead when thanking people you know only slightly. Send handwritten note cards to thank those with whom you are more familiar.

When writing a thank-you letter, acknowledge in the opening sentence the service rendered. Informal greetings are best if you are writing to someone familiar. Otherwise, stick with courtesy titles ("Dear Mr. Cutler"). A thank-you letter should be sincere, as in the sample below:

Dear Rob,

On behalf of our management team, I want to thank you for all your hard work in arranging our company banquet. We were thrilled at how well it turned out.

Especially noteworthy was your team's ability to arrange for John Foster to deliver the keynote address. John's talk literally made the event. We could not have done it without your help.

Please convey our thanks to all the members of your team. I hope to call on you again for our next company gathering.

Sincerely,

Jack Caudrette

Jack Caudrette
Manager of Special Events

Refusal Letter

The refusal letter politely declines something, be it a proposition from another company or a job that has been offered to you. Think of it as a "no, thank you" letter. Always be gracious. Thank the recipient for her time or for any special arrangements or considerations that were made on your behalf. Don't waste time expressing your regrets. State the reason that you won't be taking the recipient up on the offer. A long explanation isn't necessary, but saying something about how you arrived at your decision is often a good idea. Close the letter congenially by reinforcing your gratitude and conveying your best wishes. A refusal letter should sound something like this:

Dear Ms. Jordan,

We appreciate your interest in the position of circulation manager at Zelda Publishing. Although your qualifications are excellent, we have hired a candidate who has stronger experience with Internet advertising, our current focus.

We gave careful consideration to this decision because of the strength of your overall experience. We will keep your credentials on file in the event a position opens in the future.

Please accept our best wishes for your job search.

Sincerely,

Michelle Lowenstein

Michelle Lowenstein
Circulation Development Manager

• POWER POINTS •

THE WRITING MANAGER

Managers who write successfully adhere to principles that get proven business results:

- Write a "grabber"—an opening sentence that compels people to keep reading.

- Pinpoint specific benefits they can offer their audience.

- Provide evidence of such benefits to bolster their claims.

- Solicit feedback from their colleagues.

Refusal letters mark you as a true professional. The courteousness and honesty of your refusal letter—even when the news is disappointing—will leave the recipient with a favorable impression, which may stand you in good stead in the future.

Letters of Request

Letters that make a claim on another's time or resources require some thought before they are written. Typically they should be short and include an introduction, the actual request, and information on how to reach you.

Sometimes letters of request serve a more thorny function, such as collecting on overdue

Dos & Don'ts ☑

ASKING FAVORS

Request letters require extra measures of tact and courtesy.

- ☐ Don't sound cloying or insincere.
- ☐ Do be candid about your reason for writing.
- ☐ Do be brief.
- ☐ Don't give a hard sell.
- ☐ Don't sound too confident or optimistic.
- ☐ Don't make unrealistic requests.
- ☐ Do relate the request to the person's interests.
- ☐ Don't manipulate or flatter.
- ☐ Do thank the recipients for their time and consideration.

invoices or communicating unwelcome news. These letters should be courteously formal, albeit imbued with a sense of the gravity of the situation. The objective is to state your meaning precisely. A reader should not be left to infer your intention, nor should your letter contain implied threats or sound confrontational. Here's an example of an effective letter of request:

Dear Mr. Green:

Our accounts show you have an outstanding balance of $155,372.56 covering the last six-month period. Please remit payment as soon as possible so we may continue providing uninterrupted service. If you have already sent us payment in full, please disregard this letter.

Kind regards,

Clara Smith

Clara Smith
Customer Service Manager

Note that the writer gives enough information to help Mr. Green grasp the situation and what is at stake. Without implying any threat, the letter explicitly requests that Mr. Green urgently respond by making payment. It underscores the urgency of the situation without issuing an ultimatum. Assuming Mr. Green values this writer's business, the letter may prod him to settle the account.

Letters of Complaint

Complaint letters should be reserved for communicating grievances outside your company—that is, with vendors, suppliers, or anyone your firm depends on for services or products. Should you need to lodge a complaint by letter, approach the task with caution. Writing an inflammatory letter may only compound the problem.

In the opening paragraph emphasize the positive; for example, point out that you are a longtime customer who has always been satisfied with the company's products or services. This provides a powerful fulcrum for the next paragraph, in which you introduce your complaint and include any information about the product or service, such as model number, warranty status, place of purchase, and how much you paid.

As a manager, use situations like this to build bridges rather than burn them. Not only are you solving practical business problems, but you are setting an example of leadership for others to follow.

GO RIGHT TO THE TOP

Some people consider addressing a complaint letter directly to a company's chief executive officer a break of protocol. Ellen Phillips, author of *Shocked, Appalled and Dismayed,* however, isn't among them. She advises letter-writers to target decision-makers who have the authority to actually grant what you request. Another suggestion: Send copies of your complaint letter to any relevant consumer agencies.

THE BOTTOM LINE

Letters of Apology

Never be afraid to acknowledge mistakes. Circumstances behind apologies can vary—from missing a project deadline, to sending inferior merchandise, to overcharging customers. Whatever the circumstance, apologizing will engender stronger business relationships. People are apt to forgive honest mistakes and believe most people want to remedy their failings.

First, send your apology as soon as possible. Take responsibility for what happened. Apology letters should acknowledge failings and express sincere regret, though sometimes a personal phone call may be more efficient.

Responses should be phrased as simply and concisely as possible. Be humble. Let the reader know you recognize her disappointment and vow to do better. Ask what you can do to rebuild

• POWER POINTS •

SAYING YOU'RE SORRY

Managers may have to do damage control with customers who are dissatisfied. Here is how to start when communicating regret:

- Acknowledge

- Apologize

- Ameliorate

- Ask for feedback

The BIG Picture

BUSINESS WRITING GONE AWRY

Jargon and lingo are rapidly overtaking business writing. For example, companies refer to software products as "solutions"—without first describing the problem the software needs to solve. The profusion of new technologies has also introduced a spate of acronyms and unfamiliar terminology, most of which is not readily understood by all businesspeople. The immediacy of electronic communications is also changing the rules of what is acceptable grammar and spelling.

When writing letters, ferret out any unneeded or confusing terminology. Use words that people will understand. Rather than filling your letter with jargon, speak plainly, as if you were explaining something to someone who knows nothing about the subject. Eliminate buzzwords that obscure or confuse your meaning. You can't get people interested if they don't understand what you are saying.

that person's trust. Finally, outline the steps you will take to prevent the problem next time. The apology should aim to solve a complaint and put the matter to rest.

Write your letter from the heart and close by thanking the reader for his patience and continued support as you institute these changes.

Writing about and to Employees

During your managerial career you will be called on to write letters of commendation, letters of recommendation, and letters of reprimand.

Letters of commendation. These letters praise individuals or groups who have made outstanding contributions. They are usually brief—no more than a few paragraphs—and often are presented as certificates of achievement or special awards. Letters of commendation are often taken

---

Behind the Numbers

KEEP IT SHORT

Longer sentences tend to make readers' minds wander. According to the *Kansas City Star,* research shows that readers' comprehension drops with longer sentences.

When reading sentences of 15 words or fewer, readers comprehend 90 percent. When reading sentences of 25 words or more, readers comprehend 62 percent. The lesson? Always use shorter, punchier sentences to help readers get your meaning—and get it quickly.

SOURCE: "When You Write, Do It Right" by Diane Stafford, *Kansas City Star* (June 20, 2004).

---

into account when determining merit raises and promotions, so it's critical that managers learn to write them well. Consider the following example of a commendation letter written by a manager at a large manufacturer praising the work of a smaller construction firm hired to complete a project:

Dear Mr. White,

I want to thank you for the impeccable job your crew did on our new manufacturing plant.

We are thrilled with the quality of the construction and are especially grateful for your team's diligence in keeping the project on budget and on time, despite this summer's rainy weather. I also want to recognize your safety performance. Your crew completed the entire project, stretching over a year, with no injuries. This is to be highly commended.

It was a pleasure dealing with you. Please pass along our gratitude to Crew Supervisors Bob Balboa and Stan Rufus, and, of course, to your top-notch construction team.

Sincerely,

Jeff Groundstone

Jeff Groundstone
Project Manager

Letters of recommendation. If you are sorry to be losing an employee, let that be reflected in the quality of the recommendation you write. Make sure you write not only about the person's technical skills and competence, but also about his or her personal qualities (trustworthiness,

> "A writer, writing away, can always fix himself up to make himself more presentable, but a man who has written a letter is stuck with it for all time."
>
> —E. B. White,
> coauthor of *The Elements of Style*
> (1899–1985)

ability to work well with others, etc.). If you are writing a letter for someone whose contributions won't be missed, focus on the person's strengths.

If an employee asks for a letter of recommendation for a specific purpose, ask the employee for the name and title of the person to whom it should be addressed. Often, however, employees will request a letter of recommendation that they can present to prospective employers in the future. In this case, it is okay to use the impersonal

"To whom it may concern" in the greeting. Below is an example of a solid recommendation:

To Whom It May Concern:

I highly recommend Doug Kearns as a candidate for employment. Doug was employed by American Pharmaceuticals Company from March 2002 to February 2006.

Doug was responsible for payment application and collections of approximately 350 accounts with balances in excess of $25 million. One of Doug's largest accounts was the U.S. Department of Defense. His responsibilities included calculating and charging late fees, calculating interest on notes, and providing customer support. He was able to achieve outstanding success in collecting delinquent balances.

Doug is a good communicator who is organized, efficient, and reliable. He can work independently, is able to follow through, and is always flexible. Doug would be a tremendous asset for any company he joins and has my highest recommendation.

Sincerely,

Burton Lawler

Burton Lawler
Regional Accounts Receivables Manager

Letters of reprimand. These difficult letters are used for disciplinary purposes related to policy violations or subpar performance. Reprimands lay out corrective actions that the employee must take, timetables for review, and the consequences if the employee doesn't improve. When writing letters of reprimand, focus on specific actions or behaviors that need to change, rather than on a person's attitude.

THE REPORT

Reports are lengthy documents typically written to inform or apprise readers of a situation and recommend future steps. They often serve as sources for informed decision-making, so accuracy and clarity are paramount.

Reports can be produced collaboratively by a team or by a sole author. One person generally assumes the task of writing the report even if many people contribute to its creation.

A credible report is characterized by objectivity and reliance on facts. Unlike a pitch, reports make no direct attempt to sway people's opinions. They provide an overview of a topic and lay out the pros and cons. Reports make frequent use of charts, tables, and other illustrations to buttress information in the text. Some include appendixes that list reference material or sources and glossaries that define unfamiliar terminology.

Purpose and Audience

The first step in writing a report is to identify a clear purpose: Is the report needed merely

to inform people about new developments?
Is it meant to be an educational tool for people unfamiliar with the subject? Or are you attempting to shed light on an especially thorny business problem?

If you are unsure, ask your superior or the person who requested the report to clarify their expectations. Find out what information they need and why they need it. Ask explicit questions and urge people to provide as much information as possible.

Once you clarify the purpose of the report, determine your audience's expectations and knowledge base. If you are preparing a research report for people who are not experts in your field, simplify complex terms and translate

● POWER POINTS ●

THE PURPOSE-DRIVEN REPORT

A report may serve one primary purpose or several. Here are some of the most common goals of formal reports:

- To educate on a topic

- To recommend solutions to a business problem

- To explore or examine new business initiatives or opportunities

- To disseminate important information

> "Say all you have to say in the fewest possible words, or your reader will be sure to skip them; and in the plainest possible words or he will certainly misunderstand them."
>
> —John Ruskin,
> English art critic, author, and artist
> (1819–1900)

technical language into layman's language. Readers' minds may wander if the report gets bogged down in minutiae.

Research

Reports depend on facts and can entail painstaking research. You will need to familiarize yourself with previously published literature on your subject, analyze the information, and be prepared to explain it to readers. Your job is to juxtapose internal findings against existing research, giving readers perspective on how those findings fit into the "big picture."

Research data used in reports often is found within the walls of your organization. Perhaps your company has been tracking industry trends on the impact of human resources outsourcing. If so, previous studies or other in-house research probably exists. Harness these resources and augment them with new information from surveys, interviews, and white papers.

Carefully document any sources you plan to use. These will be assembled later into an appendix that cites the references you consulted. Citing other people's work on the subject lets people know you have done your homework—not to mention guards against charges you plagiarized someone else's work.

Once you have finished your research, break down your notes into chunks of related information and analyze your findings. Organize a rough outline of your report based on these findings. An outline will give you a sense of how the document will look and help you assess its length.

Writing and Organizing the Report

Once you've completed your research, you are ready to begin writing. First establish the organizing principle you will build the report around. There may be several themes you wish to address. If that's the case, you will have to decide which theme takes precedence and which ones have lower priority.

Introduction. Begin by describing the subject of the report, giving background information, and stating the purpose of your report. The introduction should be brief and succinct and

POWER POINTS

WRITING THE RIGHT REPORT

Countless business reports are generated each year. Companies use the information in these reports to monitor the competition and seek new opportunities. Common types of business reports include:

- Sales forecasts
- Marketing studies
- Initiative proposals
- Progress reports
- Industry surveys
- Technical reports
- Feasibility studies
- Financial reports

should draw the reader into the report. The body of the report will flesh out the key points described in the introduction.

Body of the report. This is the part in which you turn information into knowledge. Whenever possible, organize the body of the report into several sections and, if appropriate, divide each section into subsections. Each section should be given a brief but informative heading, each subsection a subheading. The use of

Dos & Don'ts ☑

REPORT WRITING

When writing reports, remember to pay special attention to style, language, tone, and form:

☐ Do use precise language.

☐ Don't be condescending.

☐ Do create a pithy executive summary.

☐ Do write in a conversational tone.

☐ Don't barrage readers with highly technical terms.

☐ Do include an appendix or glossary when appropriate.

☐ Do attribute sources of research in a bibliography, footnotes, or endnotes.

headings and subheadings lends coherence to the overall document and helps readers follow the structure of the report. Headings also serve as visual guides that help readers decide which information is relevant to them and which can be skipped. For instance, for a report on how to boost your company's presence in the market, you might organize the body of the report in this way:

1. Obstacles to Market Penetration
   a. The Market Is Saturated
      Explain the causes
   b. New Competitors Have Emerged
      Identify them and their products
   c. Customer Demands Are Evolving
      Consider if we are nimble enough to respond
2. Strategies for Gaining Market Share
   a. Build on Customer Loyalty
      Offer special pricing and incentives
   b. Exploit Our Size and Entrepreneurial Nature
      Attract smaller companies
   c. Diversify Our Offerings
      Recommend other services we can offer

Keep the writing pithy yet conversational, but let objectivity be your guiding principle. Your goal is to equip readers with factual information, so do not include your personal feelings about the topic. If your views are important to the discussion, distinguish opinions from empirical data with separate headings or appropriate subheadings.

The conclusion. Although limited to a few hundred words, the conclusion packs a wallop: It summarizes the points and findings presented in the body of the report, assesses their implications, and determines if further research is warranted. The conclusion is not the place to introduce new information. It often includes recommendations or requests for action.

WORK **FLOW** TOOLS

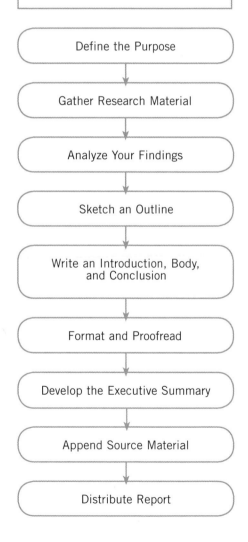

WRITING A REPORT

Define the Purpose

Gather Research Material

Analyze Your Findings

Sketch an Outline

Write an Introduction, Body, and Conclusion

Format and Proofread

Develop the Executive Summary

Append Source Material

Distribute Report

Dos & Don'ts ☑

A-PLUS REPORTS

Amid the flood of information and research involved in preparing a report, don't lose sight of a few basic principles:

☐ Do sketch out an outline of the report before you write it.

☐ Do use brief but informative headings and subheadings.

☐ Don't overwhelm readers with too many graphics.

☐ Do write your executive summary last.

☐ Don't forget to cite sources for your material.

☐ Do allot enough time to carefully edit and proofread your report.

List each recommendation separately, along with its potential benefits and drawbacks.

Although it appears at the end, many people find it helpful to write the conclusion first. It can help you pinpoint any gaps in logic or points that need to be fleshed out in the body.

Executive summary. Having laid out your case for action in the conclusion, the last thing you should write is the most important element of the report: the executive summary. Also called an abstract, an executive summary actually appears at the beginning of the report. Typically no longer than 250 to 300 words, it is usually the most

> "Vigorous writing is concise. A sentence should contain no unnecessary words, a paragraph no unnecessary sentences, for the same reason that a drawing should have no unnecessary lines and a machine no unnecessary parts. "
>
> —William Strunk, Jr., coauthor of *The Elements of Style* (1869–1946)

difficult part of the report to write. Unlike the introduction, the executive summary doesn't merely outline the points covered in the report, but also includes analysis and foreshadows your conclusions or recommendations.

Outside the Box

THE LOWDOWN ON WHITE PAPERS

Reports are often confused with white papers. But white papers are actually slightly different from internal corporate reports. They are designed for consumption by industry analysts, prospective customers, professional associations, academics, journalists, and other people who might need the information. Companies don't charge people to read their white papers; in fact, they often distribute them for free on the Internet or by other means.

White papers give managers a chance to share their expertise and strengthen their companies' position in the market. A white paper usually is geared to a specific audience of like-minded people and can be used to both inform and persuade. Writing a white paper, either alone or as part of a group, is a way to polish your skills and expand your reputation.

The people reading your report may be extremely busy. Many of them, in fact, will read only the executive summary and the conclusion. So allot plenty of time to writing, revising, and editing these two sections, as they will get the most intensive attention.

Appendixes. An appendix is any supplementary material attached at the end of a document for reference. The two most common appendixes are bibliographies and glossaries.

> "A scrupulous writer, in every sentence that he writes, will ask himself at least four questions, thus: 1. What am I trying to say? 2. What words will express it? 3. What image or idiom will make it clearer? 4. Is this image fresh enough to have an effect?"
>
> —George Orwell,
> English novelist and journalist
> (1903–1950)

A bibliography lists the works that were consulted in preparing the report. Each entry includes the title of the source, name of its

• POWER POINTS •

DON'T REMOVE YOUR APPENDIX

An appendix comprises supplemental information about primary sources cited in the report. Items typically include:

- Photographs
- Illustrations
- Maps
- Diagrams
- Surveys
- Statistical abstracts
- Calculations/formulas

author, publisher, and publication date. The bibliography guides readers to further reading relevant to the subject of the report.

A glossary is a list of technical terms, abbreviations, acronyms, and their meaning. Glossaries are particularly important in reports on complex, technical topics that will be distributed to nontechnical readers.

Crediting sources. If your report includes verbatim quotes or paraphrased passages from other material, you must acknowledge your sources. Failing to do so is committing plagiarism—the act of passing off someone else's ideas or words

Dos & Don'ts ☑

GRAB 'EM WITH GRAPHICS

☐ Do use graphics to illustrate and clarify major points in the body of your report.

☐ Don't introduce new material or make a new point with a graphic.

☐ Don't use illustrations or images simply to fill up space.

☐ Do use color selectively.

☐ Don't forget to acknowledge the source of the graphic or data illustrated.

as your own. For instance, if you include a verbatim quote or paraphrased comment attributed to Microsoft founder Bill Gates, you must acknowledge Gates as the original source for this quote or comment either in the text or in a footnote or endnote.

Footnotes appear at the bottom of the page in which the source is cited. Endnotes list all the sources used in the report in a separate section at the end of a document. To find out how to cite sources correctly and consistently, check a standard style guide, such as *The Chicago Manual of Style.* Most word-processing programs have functions that allow you to insert and keep track of footnotes and endnotes.

POWER POINTS

HITTING THE MARK

To ensure your report is well received and promptly read by your audience, follow some of these tips:

- Give it a compelling and catchy title.

- Include an executive summary of your findings so readers can scan the highlights.

- Use graphic elements such as charts and tables to illustrate key information and enliven your report.

- Clarify how the findings in the report are relevant to your organization and make appropriate recommendations in the conclusion.

- Make sure the report is properly formatted and that there aren't any glaring typos or errors.

Appearance Is Everything

How you present information is often as important as the quality of information you provide. Readers are likely to discredit or dismiss your report if it looks carelessly done or sloppy.

Prepare your reports on 8½-by-11 paper. Set standard margins, and follow a block text format: flush your paragraphs left, don't use indentations, and leave a line space between paragraphs. Consistency is key: Make sure all your headings and subheadings are formatted uniformly. If you are using bulleted or numbered lists, make sure these are done consistently as well.

Help readers grasp your data by sprinkling the report with informative graphics such as pie charts, illustrations, and tables. In addition to giving readers a breather from the text, graphics provide a lot of information at a glance.

If your report relies heavily on graphic elements, it may be best to present them in a separate appendix. However you choose to do it, clearly mark each illustration for easy reference (for example, "Figure 3: Year by Year Revenue of the Top Five HR Outsourcing Providers").

The standard layout of a report is as follows:
- Cover page
- Executive summary
- Table of contents
- Introduction
- Body of the report
- Conclusion
- Appendixes

Editing and Proofreading

Once you are through writing the report, rigorously proofread it. Look for ways to tighten up the writing or to inject life into "dead spots." Give copies of the report to a few people you trust, preferably those with knowledge of the subject matter, and request their feedback on possible changes.

Ask them to point out inconsistencies and suggest ways of making the report clearer and more comprehensible. This also is the time to double-check the spelling of all proper names in the report: people, companies, organizations, institutions, and trademark names. You don't want to mistake, say, Acme Co., which makes batteries, for Acme Corp., which sells women's apparel. The number of mistakes and typos you catch will increase in direct proportion to the number of people who review it with a critical eye before it is distributed.

RECORDING MEETING MINUTES

Occasionally, you may be asked to record formal and informal minutes of business meetings. Although this task is often viewed as mere clerical duty, the person taking and transcribing the notes functions, in essence, as a historian. You are capturing the proceedings of a meeting so people who did not attend can find out what took place in their absence. Unlike other business documents, minutes should be free of persuasion, opinion, or analysis.

When taking notes, don't try to write down exactly what a person said, but rather take simple notes using your own shorthand. Substitute figures and letters for words, such as "$" to denote dollars or money. Whichever method you choose, place a premium on legibility, and type your handwritten notes immediately after the meeting.

• POWER POINTS •

MINUTES BASICS

If called on to take the minutes of a meeting, you'll draw on two facets of communication: listening and writing.

- Listen attentively.

- Use shorthand to take notes.

- Transcribe immediately.

- Proofread and edit.

- Distribute the minutes.

Organizing and Formatting Minutes

Minutes follow a straightforward format. Most meetings at which minutes are required use a formal agenda that identifies the topics to be discussed. The full title of the meeting—for example, "Weekly Marketing Meeting," "Staff Meeting"—is followed by the date, time, and place of the meeting. Next, list in alphabetical order whoever is present at the meeting.

The body of the minutes should record the actual proceedings of the meeting. Summarize what was discussed: what the key points were, what seemed to be the consensus, and what issues sparked disagreements. Don't record every word that was said or produce a "play by play" of who said what. Instead, capture the spirit of the conversation and record any resolutions or recommended actions. If several items or issues were discussed, organize the notes into several corresponding headings. Headings enable readers to quickly scan the finished document for items that most interest them. If the meeting closely followed the agenda provided in advance, use it as a guide to organize your notes.

Before distributing the minutes, proofread them carefully. As with all business writing, strive for accuracy, clarity, and simplicity.

ORAL COMMUNICATION

"It's phenomenal what openness and communication can produce. The possibilities of truly significant gain, of significant improvement are so real that it's worth the risk such openness entails."

—Stephen R. Covey, author of *The 7 Habits of Highly Effective People*

Communicating clearly in one-on-one discussions demonstrates to your employees that you are both in touch and available. Given the digital world in which we live, it is often tempting to "hide" behind technology and not communicate with people on a one-to-one basis.

Yet personal interaction is often how truly effective business relationships are born. Managers need to cultivate their speaking skills in order to articulate ideas to both individuals and groups.

THE NONVERBAL NEXUS

How do other people "read" your tone of voice or body language? Your gestures, facial expressions, movement, and body posture are all nonverbal cues that express what words might not. Smiles and an extended hand, for example, signal openness. Frowning or being too serious, on the other hand, might suggest you are inapproachable, moody, or uninterested.

Nonverbal signals can be misinterpreted however. Emphatic gestures can be misconstrued as expressing anger or dismissiveness. If your facial expression never changes—which can in fact be a sign of focused attention—some people may think you have "tuned out." Poor posture may suggest that you lack confidence or don't believe what you say—an interpretation that may harm your credibility. Many people are in the habit of folding their arms, but this gesture is often viewed as a sign of disagreement, resistance, or lack of openness.

In short, nonverbal signals say volumes about your interest in what the other person is saying. The best form of nonverbal communication is listening attentively to what others say.

ONE-ON-ONE DISCUSSIONS

Communicating with employees is a two-way street. Aside from showing respect for their opinions and ideas, inviting feedback from employees keeps you in the loop.

Let employees know you have an "open door" policy for them to voice frustrations, concerns,

NONVERBAL NO-NO'S

Posture, facial expressions, and gestures often send messages. These nonverbal signals indicate indifference or lack of interest:

- Folded arms

- Hands shoved in pockets

- Fidgeting

- Fiddling with pens, pencils

- Tapping your fingers or glancing at your watch

- Rolling your eyes

- Yawning

- Checking e-mail during face-to-face conversations

- Slouching

- Propping feet on desks, chairs

- Cleaning your glasses, or engaging in similar distracting tasks

THE BOTTOM LINE

• POWER POINTS •

POSITIVE NONVERBAL SIGNALS

Using nonverbal along with verbal communication emphasizes your interest in what others are saying. Desirable nonverbal attributes include:

- Hands at sides, on desk, on chin
- Steady eye contact
- Smiles, nods
- Changing expressions
- Not allowing interruptions
- Eliminating background noise and distractions
- Turning off cell phones, pagers, PDAs
- Listening and acknowledging verbally

and expectations. Convene a meeting with employees to generate feedback. Not only does this produce terrific ideas, it also reinforces to employees that their efforts are appreciated by their bosses.

By developing and emphasizing verbal communication, you contribute to your company. Employees are more likely to want to work for you and to respect you. You will be viewed as having credibility and integrity.

Giving Feedback

At no time are communication skills more critical than when you are offering feedback to your employees. Regular feedback creates a sense of camaraderie between managers and the workforce. Workers are more willing to go the extra mile for managers they view as supportive and interested in their daily work. The more employees understand their responsibilities and the goals you have set for them, the harder they will work to attain them.

> "Without credible communication, and a lot of it, employee hearts and minds are never captured."
>
> —John P. Kotter,
> author of *Leading Change*

A manager should speak with precision when giving feedback, setting expectations, and coaching employees. Strive to be specific with your comments rather than general. Telling someone they did a "fine job" makes them feel better but won't help employees zero in on what they did well or help them replicate that positive performance in the future.

Instead, give specifics when discussing performance and tasks with employees. For example, you might say: "Jeff, your work on this project has been superb. I know you've met tight deadlines before, so you're an old hand at this, but how close are we to the next milestone? We have about a week to go. Is there some way I can help?"

The above message conveys a challenge (tight deadline) and expresses confidence that Jeff will meet it nonetheless. The manager also offers to help, showing no reluctance to get his hands dirty.

The number-one impact that managers have on their companies is the ability to win the

Behind the Numbers

MORE FEEDBACK

Employees value regular feedback from superiors. A 2006 study by Jack Morton Worldwide, a marketing agency, found that 67 percent of employees are dissatisfied with the quality and frequency of feedback they get from their bosses. Of that number, 31 percent bluntly stated that their management doesn't communicate with them often enough.

SOURCE: "Customers or Employees First," Jack Morton Worldwide (September 25, 2006).

WIN THEIR RESPECT

A huge factor in communicating effectively is winning the respect of your employees. You can accomplish this in a number of ways:

- **Let employees finish their remarks** – Sometimes employees need to blow off a little steam. Don't become impatient with them or interrupt them.

- **Don't be an absentee manager** – You can't communicate if you aren't regularly in contact with employees. Make a point to schedule team meetings at least once a month and, if possible, meet individually with key employees on a regular basis.

- **Practice what you preach** – If you are touting the need to develop corporate values, be sure you don't violate those values yourself.

- **Be specific** – Your employees won't respect you if you are unable to clearly express ideas in team meetings. Be precise with your words, eliminating needless jargon.

THE BOTTOM LINE

CASE *FILE*

SLOGANS AT WORK

During the 2003–4 National Hockey League season, Tampa Bay Lightning head coach John Tortorella continually sounded one theme: "Good is the enemy of great." The phrase is the first line of the book *Good to Great: Why Some Companies Make the Leap . . . And Others Don't* by Jim Collins.

The book affected Tortorella so strongly that he used that first sentence as a rallying cry for his young team. Time and again, he hammered home the danger of settling for "good enough." The six-word slogan adorned banners that hung from the rafters of the Lightning's arena. Fans began wearing T-shirts and caps bearing the trademark phrase. Tortorella's insistence that his team strive for greatness paid great dividends: The team won its first Stanley Cup championship later that year. Tortorella understood the message he wanted to deliver and, like all successful mangers, distilled it into a memorable expression that yielded tangible results.

SOURCE: "Tortorella Raises Bar, Bolts Drink from Cup" by Joey Johnston, *Tampa Tribune* (June 10, 2004).

confidence of employees through credible, consistent face-to-face communication. Thus, offer feedback frequently. Don't relegate it to quarterly or yearly performance reviews.

Offering Praise and Encouragement

It's important to provide not only clear direction on work projects, but also encouraging words and praise for a job well done. Recognizing employees' efforts and accomplishments is a hallmark of strong leadership: It breeds more loyal and productive workers and sets your firm apart as a desirable place to work. It also helps keep turnover low. You will be surprised what a few words of thanks can do.

When the time comes to thank employees, be sure to do so publicly in front of their peers. This holds true whether it is an individual or a team that is being recognized. Acknowledge all contributions to a project, however small. At a meeting, you might say something like, "Janet Peterson brought to our attention that the color registration was off on the new brochure. Thanks, Janet, for catching that before we sent them out."

Shining the spotlight on employees for a few minutes gives them immense satisfaction and instills a sense of pride in their achievement. Moreover, the value these public displays serve in motivating other employees is immeasurable.

Providing Constructive Criticism

Most employees welcome constructive feedback. Diligent workers usually will respond favorably to negative feedback if it is relayed in a supportive, understanding manner. At times, your words need to reprove or warn those who aren't pulling their weight. Even here, your words should not sting but rather serve as motivators.

When delivering criticism, adopt a neutral tone and focus on the person's behavior and performance rather than attitude. Stress your willingness to help this person succeed. Offer training or other resources at your disposal that could deepen the employee's knowledge and skill base.

If your input is meant to bring about a change in behavior, target the results you want to see. You may want to ask the person if you can make a suggestion as opposed to giving a directive.

"The resentment that criticism engenders can demoralize employees, family members, and friends, and still not correct the situation that has been condemned."

—Dale Carnegie,
author of *How to Win Friends and Influence People*
(1888–1955)

Dos & Don'ts ☑

ACCEPTING CRITICISM

Graciously accepting constructive criticism from others will help you polish your rough edges and become a respected communicator.

- ☐ Do listen with an open mind.
- ☐ Don't let your ego get in the way.
- ☐ Do restate the criticism you hear.
- ☐ Don't react defensively.
- ☐ Do ask clarifying questions and for examples.
- ☐ Don't raise your voice.

Suggestions enable employees to learn new ways of doing things. "That screen might hold better if you used a bigger screw" is more useful feedback than telling someone, "The screen is falling out. Fix it." A typical conversation might go like this:

John, the manager: Hey, Tamara, may I make a suggestion?

Tamara: Sure. Go ahead.

John: Please don't misunderstand me. We all love your enthusiasm for this project and the ideas you bring to the table. Don't ever lose that. On the other hand, your ideas might get taken more seriously if you didn't interrupt so often when others were speaking.

Tamara: Wow, I wasn't aware I did that. Thanks for pointing it out. I'll try not to.

Naturally, suggestions tend to be better received than orders. Even when giving directives, keep an open mind to employees' suggestions. This may not always be possible, but you should strive to build an atmosphere of trust and mutual communication.

Soliciting Feedback

Accomplished managers must not only be able to give feedback to employees. It is sometimes helpful to solicit it from them.

If you are comfortable doing so, tell those you manage that you are open to receiving constructive criticism on how you can do your job better. Most employees would never dream of approaching the boss to offer criticism, but letting people know your door—and more important, your mind—is always open encourages trust and candor.

Absorb employees' comments in an impartial manner. If, after listening to feedback, you aren't persuaded by an argument, explain why. Regardless of whether you agree or not, tell the individual that you appreciate honest feedback, and invite a continued dialogue in the future.

Of course, the best way to defuse criticism is to stay on top of things. Talk often with employees about jobs or long-range projects. Repeatedly ask if they have everything they need to do their jobs. Solicit their feedback on ways things can be improved. Former New York City mayor Ed Koch understood this principle. "How am I

CASE *FILE*

SHOWING EMOTION

When he was CEO of optical retail chain LensCrafters, Dave Browne concedes he was a "numbers-only guy." He believed concrete facts should be used to drive business decisions.

Yet Browne eventually realized that facts and numbers can keep leaders from communicating "on a much higher plane, emotionally and with vision." So he convened an off-site meeting with employees and apologized for focusing solely on the bottom line to the exclusion of addressing employees' fears and apprehensions. Browne learned to communicate honestly and emotionally with employees—not an easy thing to do for a top executive.

"When you start sharing dreams and fears and talking about things at an emotional level," Browne concluded, "you are risking vulnerability. But it's worth it."

SOURCE: "Is One-Dimensional Communication Limiting Your Leadership?" by Theodore Kinni, *Harvard Management Communication Letter* (May 2003).

doing?" Koch famously would ask when shaking hands with people all around the city. Asking for regular feedback will help you become a more responsive and capable leader.

Discussing Employees' Performance

If an employee's performance starts to lag, the first step is to find out why. Approach the employee and honestly express your concern. Be sensitive. Avoid threats and coercion, which are the habits of bad managers and demoralize rather than motivate. Find out if personal issues are weighing on the employee's mind.

> "The most important thing in communication is hearing what isn't said."
>
> —Peter Drucker,
> management guru and author
> (1909–2005)

Remember all disciplinary discussions should revolve around performance and job goals. After you've discussed the employee's performance, wait a while—perhaps several weeks—to see if the individual turns things around. Sometimes, a word of encouragement is enough to reignite someone's commitment to the job.

If you don't see improvement, call the person in for a meeting. Let the person know in advance that you want to talk to him or her. Let the employee know you appreciate his contributions. But express your disappointment that things haven't improved. Let the person know the consequences of continuing to underperform.

A one-on-one meeting may reveal the reasons behind a person's performance lag. Perhaps all

Dos & Don'ts ☑

DELICATE DISCIPLINE

A disciplinary session with an employee will be more productive if you keep certain guidelines in mind:

☐ Do request to meet at the employee's convenience.

☐ Do use neutral language.

☐ Do lead the discussion by thanking the employee for his or her positive contributions.

☐ Do be specific about what the employee needs to do differently or what areas of competency need to be improved.

☐ Do set clear expectations for improvement.

☐ Don't threaten in fact or by implication.

☐ Do offer to train the person, if appropriate.

☐ Do keep discussions confidential.

the person needs is some focused training in a particular aspect of his job. Perhaps there are institutional roadblocks obstructing his efforts. There may be personal problems distracting the employee. In some cases, an employee genuinely could be giving his best and simply be ill-suited to his current position.

> "To succeed, you will soon learn, as I did, the importance of a solid foundation in the basics of education— literacy, both verbal and numerical, and communication skills."
>
> —Alan Greenspan, former Federal Reserve chairman

Your job is to stay abreast of the many variables that can affect workplace performance and productivity. This involves acquainting yourself with your employees' competencies and potential by committing to a policy of "open door" communications.

Still, there may be times when you will need to put your foot down. Disciplining employees is probably the most difficult task you will face as a manager. The manner in which you deliver a disciplinary message is as important as its content. Be firm and supportive at the same time. It's best to avoid ultimatums.

Firing Employees

Sometimes letting someone go is unavoidable despite your best efforts. When breaking the news to an employee, do it in private and discreetly. Summarize your reasons for dismissal, focusing on the employee's performance, not on the person.

No matter how justified the dismissal, the person is liable to be angry. Allow him to vent his feelings, but don't retreat from your stance. At all costs preserve the individual's dignity, despite any personal conflicts that may exist between the two of you. Wish him well and express your regret at needing to take such a drastic measure.

TELEPHONE: THE RULES OF ENGAGEMENT

According to a 1999 study conducted by etiquette consultant Eticon Inc., 8 out of 10 people surveyed believe rudeness in business is on the rise. Telephone manners are at the root of over 60 percent of rudeness complaints. Reviewing the following tips on proper phone manners will help you make telephone conversations more productive.

Create a good impression. Answer the phone as soon as possible, certainly after no more than three rings. Stick to a formal tone of voice during your greeting and speak slowly. Here are a few examples of professional greetings:

"This is Jeff Warmouth. How may I help you?"

"Hello, this is Jeff Warmouth speaking."

"Hello, this is Jeff. How may I help you?"

Unless directed otherwise, don't add company slogans or catchy sales phrases to your greeting. They just delay the caller from saying what he wants to say.

> # "Good manners are good business."
>
> —Nancy Mitchell,
> etiquette expert

Your attitude and mood come through loud and clear on the phone. Smile when you're talking on the phone. According to Nancy Friedman, who runs the communication training company The Telephone Doctor, callers can instantly detect a smile—as well as the lack of one. Even if you're having a bad day, never take it out on the caller.

Turn off distractions. Don't answer the phone or initiate a phone call if you are in the middle of a conversation with someone else or engaged in a meeting (unless you are bringing the caller

Dos & Don'ts ☑

VOICE-MAIL ETIQUETTE

Messages you leave should be courteous, meaningful, and to the point.

☐ Do keep it short and simple.

☐ Do speak clearly and slowly.

☐ Don't express anger or use harsh words in your message.

☐ Do leave the time and date of your message, as well as your name, the company you are calling from, and your number.

☐ Don't hang up abruptly; always thank the recipient of the message.

into a conference call with everyone present). Be considerate of others.

Don't leave them hanging. Never leave someone on hold for too long. If you must put someone on hold, please alert or ask them beforehand ("May I put you on hold for just a minute?"). After you've taken the caller off hold, make sure to thank him or her for holding. If you are not at your desk to take a phone call, respond to voice mails or messages in a timely manner, at least by the close of business that day. Instruct your staff to do the same.

Behind the Numbers

ANSWER THE PHONE—PLEASE!

According to Eticon Inc., an etiquette consultant, the three phone offenses that anger customers the most are:

Undue time on hold	27%
Unreturned calls	24%
Confusing voice-mail prompts	11%

SOURCE: "Rudeness Can Cost Business" by Jenny Munro, *The Greenville News* (October 8, 2000).

Leave clear messages. When leaving voice-mail messages, keep them simple and to the point. Identify yourself by your full name, even if you've spoken with the person before (unless, of course, the person is a colleague you talk to frequently). Provide the name of your company and your job title if necessary. Speak slowly, and enunciate. Try to keep your messages as brief as possible. They should not exceed 30 seconds. If you request a call back, leave your telephone number along with the best time to call.

Placing a difficult call. If you are about to speak with someone concerning matters that are difficult or controversial, first take the time to plan how to approach the conversation. Ask yourself: How difficult will it be for this individual to handle what I have to say? What words or approach will soften the blow?

When you do place the call, first ask if the person has time to talk with you. Without getting into specifics, let the individual know the matter requires urgent attention. If the person can't talk at the moment, schedule a time to talk later. Always keep your tone professional by speaking in a moderate voice. Be genial even while being firm. To the extent possible, don't discuss personnel matters on the phone. Try instead to meet privately with the person.

Receiving a difficult call. Answering a surprise call on a sensitive topic requires deftness and quick thinking. Usually these calls come from people who are upset about something—for example, a customer fuming over bad service or a boss delivering unexpected news. In these situations, grace under pressure serves you well.

Let the caller blow off steam, but slow the pace of the conversation by repeating what the person has said or asking for clarifications. Do your best to prevent the conversation from escalating and try not to be baited into an argument. Avoid sounding defensive. Instead, answer whatever questions you can and commit to finding answers to those you can't. Apologize for any mistakes on your or your company's part, and promise to follow up. At all costs, keep your cool. Don't try to win an argument; try to win the person over.

Receiving unwanted phone calls. Although it might be tempting to abruptly brush off cold callers or misdirected phone calls, it is never a good idea. How you handle annoying "cold calls" says a lot about your professionalism.

Dos & Don'ts ☑

CELL PHONE FAUX PAS

Cell phones have enhanced our productivity. They can become an offensive distraction, however, if used inconsiderately.

☐ Don't select whimsical ring tones; they are unprofessional.

☐ Do set the ringer to silent or vibrate if you must keep your phone on at all times for emergencies.

☐ Do turn off cell phones during meetings to prevent interruptions.

If you get a phone call that should be handled by another person or department, politely help the caller reach the intended person by supplying the name and number of the person who can help or by transferring the call.

CONFERENCE CALLS AND VIDEOCONFERENCING

Communicating with people in far-flung locations is much easier today than it was decades ago. Conference calls save you from traveling to meetings across town, or across the country. You can bring together the various parties via

- [ ] Do warn others if you are expecting a call during a meeting. Excuse yourself to another room during the call and limit your absence to only a few minutes.

- [ ] Do modulate your voice. Cell-phone technology has a more hollow sound than landlines, causing people to project their voices louder.

- [ ] Don't sneak your phone inside areas where they are banned, such as places with sensitive electronic equipment.

phone so everyone gets the information at the same time.

As companies and business go global, video-conferencing enables people to communicate with each other all over the world, using web-cams, software, and computers. They are able to see each other and exchange information just as though they were sitting across the room.

Videoconferencing is still evolving, however, and the technology is far from perfect. Software glitches and equipment failure may disrupt your videoconference, so always have a fallback plan. Participants should know beforehand what to do if the camera loses its signal or a power outage wipes out your high-speed tele-communication line.

Leading the Conference Call or Videoconference

Efficient phone and videoconferences demand organization and planning. If you are leading the conference, you will be in charge of facilitating the discussion, making sure the whole agenda is covered, and tracking time.

First, familiarize yourself thoroughly with any material up for discussion and draft an agenda

Behind the Numbers

THE VIDEOCONFERENCING TREND

Research suggests that companies are steadily increasing their use of audio and videoconferencing equipment.

Year	Sales of equipment (in billions)
2000	$2.84
2001	$3.18
2002	$3.35
2003	$3.41
2004	$3.20
2005	$3.99
2006	$4.33

SOURCE: "Conferencing Takes Wing as Travel Option" by Eric Benderoff and Mike Hughlett, *Chicago Tribune* (August 11, 2006).

● **POWER POINTS** ●

CONFERENCE PROTOCOL

Your conference call or video-conference will run much more smoothly if you adhere to a few rules:

- Ask participants to identify themselves when speaking.

- Steer the discussion to items on the agenda.

- Keep track of time.

- Allot time for questions.

- Schedule a follow-up meeting if you run out of time and don't cover all of the items on the agenda.

- Thank participants for their time and input.

if necessary. Be considerate of other people's schedules and start on time whenever possible. You may wish to wait a few minutes for everyone to join the conference, but don't hold up the call or videoconference for latecomers. Depending on the number of people and their familiarity with one another, introductions may not be needed or otherwise take only a few minutes. If you are conducting a conference call, remind people to identify themselves again should they choose to speak during the call.

Except under extreme circumstances, keep your call to the allotted time. Allocate a set number of minutes to discuss each item on your agenda, and then move to the next item. If you think the call or videoconference will run longer than expected, give participants the option of continuing the call or signing off. If by the end of the scheduled call there are still agenda items to be discussed, ask participants to schedule a follow-up call. Close the meeting by summarizing all the items that have been discussed and thanking people for their time and input.

PRESENTING IN PUBLIC

Managers who can deftly explain complicated information with a few well-turned phrases increase their chances of assuming greater responsibility. But presenting material in front of an audience—whether in a big auditorium or in a small conference room down the hall—can be intimidating. Even when speaking before people we know well, we all have experienced fluttering stomachs and sweaty palms.

The key to preparing oral presentations is to allow yourself enough time to research and digest the material you will be presenting. First sketch a bare outline of your ideas on paper and rework it until you are comfortable with it. This process is highly intuitive and likely to involve writing and revising your presentation script numerous times.

Know your audience. Learn as much about your audience as you can beforehand. Will you be presenting in front of people you know?

The **BIG** Picture

SCRIPTED OR EXTEMPORANEOUS?

Speakers with an evident command of their subject matter who appear at ease before an audience convey an added degree of authority. But not everyone can speak convincingly "off the cuff." Decide which of these two approaches best suits your public-speaking abilities.

Reading from notes or a script keeps you from digressing and preserves the continuity of your message. Following a structure helps you adhere to time limits and also reduces the chance for mistakes. The downside: Done poorly, this method fails to engage your listeners.

Speaking extemporaneously enables you to zero in on the audience, rather than fumbling through notes. Because you will appear polished and poised, people will place confidence in what you say. Caution: You must be able to do this well or risk skipping chunks of information or rambling beyond the time limit.

Does your audience share similar interests and knowledge? Will you be presenting information that many in the gathering probably have never heard about? Knowing and understanding your audience will help you adjust the content of your presentation accordingly.

Practice makes perfect. If you are new to public speaking, use a tape recorder to get comfortable hearing the sound of your own voice. Rehearse your presentation in front of friends, family members, or colleagues and ask them to critique your delivery, body language, and facial expressions. Find out if they understood the basics of your talk by asking them to summarize the main points of your presentation.

• POWER POINTS •

CALM YOUR NERVES

Toastmasters International is an organization that helps people build their public speaking skills. Here are some tips they offer for speaking in public:

- Select a topic you are knowledgeable about. You should know more about the topic than you share in your talk.

- Rehearse to reinforce. Ideally, you should practice with the equipment and tools you will be using.

- Arrive early to greet people. This is a great way to establish rapport.

Set up your props. If you will be using a laptop or any other equipment, determine ahead of time if the place where you will be giving your presentation can handle that equipment. If you are presenting at an older facility that cannot accommodate your equipment, have a backup plan that relies more heavily on handouts and visual aids.

If possible, arrive at the meeting place well ahead of time. Bring along one or two other people to assist you with technical matters, such as setting up the equipment for slide shows,

- Survey the premises. If possible, run through a quick test of your equipment and the room's acoustics.

- Visualize yourself giving the talk, including hearing the audience applaud.

- Relax. People in the crowd will be rooting for you.

- Ignore your nervousness and the audience will too.

SOURCE: "10 Tips for Successful Public Speaking" Toastmasters International, www.toastmasters.org

overhead transparencies, films, and the like. Walk around the room and get a feel for the acoustics. Test microphones, if you will be using them, to ensure they work properly. If you are using battery-powered equipment, bring extra batteries just in case.

Conduct a final check. Use whatever spare time you have to perform a practice run through your presentation. Check one last time for any factual errors in your presentation script and slides. Arriving early will also give you an opportunity to "meet and greet" some of the attendees. Looking around the room during your talk and seeing familiar faces will give you a sense of rapport with those who have come to hear you speak.

Ease into your talk. When you deliver the presentation, stand squarely and face the audience. Take a deep breath. Smile. Clearly state your name and summarize your professional credentials. Welcome everyone and thank them for attending. If you are providing handouts, take a moment to ensure everyone has them. You are now ready to delve into the substance of your talk. If you're stuck for an opener, lighthearted personal anecdotes are tried-and-true tools to get the crowd on your side from the start.

Avoid needless digressions. Instead keep your presentation focused on a few major points. If you feel people are getting antsy, move on to the next point.

Rely on active verbs to keep the content lively. If your talk is full of coded language or obscure terms, listeners will tune you out. Provide critical analysis without sounding opinionated or preachy. Use gestures strategically to emphasize significant information.

Limit your use of visual aids to get the maximum effect. Few things bore people more quickly than a mind-numbing string of fancy graphics. Augment visual aids with printed copies of the material, so readers can follow along with you and see where you are headed.

Allot time for audience members to ask questions after your concluding remarks. Refer to this opportunity occasionally during your talk. For example: "I won't go into details now, but I will be taking questions later if any of you want me to expand on it." Comments like this arouse curiosity, get people thinking ahead, and trigger questions.

When fielding questions, don't congratulate individuals with comments such as "Great question!" This might make other people feel as though their questions are somehow less important to you. Always summarize or restate each question for those in the audience who may not have heard it.

Expect the unexpected. Equipment breaks down. Meetings start late. People talk during your presentation. These and other distractions await you, so be sure you have a backup plan in case you need to change course in midstream. Stay calm during any delays and interruptions.

Developing effective communication is a career-long journey. Once you are recognized as a master communicator, don't be surprised at being asked to take on greater responsibilities.

Off and Running >>>

You are now ready to put what you have learned from this book into practice. Use this section as a review guide:

CHAPTER 1.
COMMUNICATING CLEARLY IN WRITING

- The ability to write well is essential to advancing your managerial career.

- Research and planning is the first step to crafting a well-written message.

- Whether you are writing a brief e-mail or formal business report, correct grammar, accurate language, and good manners are critical.

- Clarity and simplicity are the cornerstone of good writing. Buzzwords and jargon should be eliminated.

- Understanding whom you are writing for and *why* you are writing—to inform or to persuade—helps target written communications more effectively.

- Revising and editing are the last—but most crucial—steps in the writing process.

CHAPTER 2.
DIGITAL COMMUNICATION

- Business e-mails should be treated with the same care as other forms of written communication: attention to details and grammar is paramount.

- The rules of e-mail etiquette are simple: be courteous, reply to e-mails promptly, err on the side of a formal tone, limit use of abbreviations, double-check spelling of recipients and their addresses.

- E-mail and instant messaging should be used only for company business; employees should be discouraged from sending and receiving personal or inappropriate e-mails at work.

CHAPTER 3.
PRECISION ON PAPER

- Internal memorandums, or memos, are brief documents used to impart information within a select group of people.

- Memos consist of a heading—date, recipients, sender, and subject line— and a body of text.

Off and Running >>>

- All business letters are formal by nature and are generally written either to notify, request, respond, or persuade.

- An effective business letter is well structured—with a proper greeting, body of text and closing—and correctly formatted (either in block format or modified block format).

- Reports are formal, lengthy documents drafted to inform readers, apprise them of a current situation, or recommend actions.

- A credible report is characterized by objectivity and reliance on facts.

- Recorded meeting minutes should be free of persuasion, opinion, or analysis, and should be accurate, succinct, and straightforward.

CHAPTER 4.
ORAL COMMUNICATION

- It is essential for managers to cultivate good speaking skills.

- Nonverbal cues, such as your gestures, facial expressions, and posture, express what your words might not.

- The best form of nonverbal communication is to listen attentively.

- At no time are communication skills more critical than when you are giving feedback to an employee.

- Answering the phone and leaving voice-mail messages requires politeness and professionalism at all times.

- The key to oral presentations is thorough preparation. Write, revise, and practice your script.

Recommended Reading

How to Win Friends and Influence People
Dale Carnegie
First published in 1937, this influential book offers time-honored advice on doing just what it says, proving that influencing other people in a positive manner can help you succeed in just about every endeavor.

Creativity: Flow and the Psychology of Discovery and Invention
Dr. Mihaly Csikszentmihalyi
Drawing on 100 interviews with exceptional people, from biologists and physicists to politicians and business leaders, poets and artists, as well as his thirty years of research on the subject, acclaimed psychologist Csikszentmihalyi explores the creative process.

Flow: The Psychology of Optimal Experience
Dr. Mihaly Csikszentmihalyi
This best-selling introduction to Dr. Csikszentmihalyi's landmark "flow" theory presents interviews with almost 100 creative people from a wide array of fields, exploring the creative process and showing the benefits of creative thinking on one's quality of life.

The 7 Habits of Highly Effective People: Powerful Lessons in Personal Change
Stephen R. Covey
First published in 1990, this best seller shows you how

to change your mindset to adopt these important habits for success. Translated into 32 languages, this book has sold more than 10 million copies.

The Daily Drucker: 366 Days of Insight and Motivation for Getting the Right Things Done
Peter F. Drucker with Joseph A. Maciariello
Widely regarded as the greatest management thinker of modern times, Drucker here offers his penetrating and practical wisdom with his trademark clarity, vision, and humanity. *The Daily Drucker* provides the inspiration and advice to meet life's many challenges.

The Effective Executive
Peter F. Drucker
Drucker shows how to "get the right things done," demonstrating the distinctive skill of the executive and offering fresh insights into old and seemingly obvious business situations.

Handbook of Business Letters
L. E. Frailey
Originally published in 1970, long before e-mail came on the scene, this classic book helps you write professional letters, offering models of correspondence for every occasion.

How to Talk So People Listen: Connecting in Today's Workplace
Sonya Hamlin
One of the country's leading communicators delivers groundbreaking insights and solutions to some of today's major communication issues at work: negotiating the generation gaps, integrating a multicultural workforce, organizing your message and making it visual, and understanding what motivates today's audiences.

Executive Intelligence: What All Great Leaders Have
Justin Menkes
In this thought-provoking volume, Menkes pinpoints the cognitive skills needed to thrive in senior management positions.

*Speak Without Fear: A Total System for Becoming a
Natural, Confident Communicator*
Ivy Naistadt
This guide to combating stage fright in everyday business
situations will help you become a natural, confident
communicator.

*Simply Speaking: How to Communicate Your Ideas with
Style, Substance and Clarity*
Peggy Noonan
Best-selling author, columnist, and presidential
speechwriter Peggy Noonan shares her valuable
experiences from years in the White House speech-
writing trenches, offering specific techniques, fascinating
anecdotes, and professional secrets of the trade.

*In Search of Excellence: Lessons from America's Best-
Run Companies*
Thomas J. Peters and Robert H. Waterman, Jr.
Based on a study of 43 of America's best-run companies
from a diverse array of business sectors, *In Search
of Excellence* describes eight basic principles of
management that made these organizations successful,
including helpful advice on communication.

*Emily Post's The Etiquette Advantage in Business, 2nd
Edition: Personal Skills for Professional Success*
Peggy Post and Peter Post
Helpful advice for appropriate behavior and
communication in both everyday and unusual situations,
this is an essential guide to professional and personal
success.

*How to Work a Room: The Ultimate Guide to Savvy
Socializing In-Person and On-Line*
Susan RoAne
"The Mingling Maven" Susan RoAne provides the tools
and techniques for savvy socializing in all situations in
order to establish connections that build personal and
professional relationships.

*Quiet Leadership: Six Steps to Transforming
Performance at Work*
David Rock
Rock demonstrates how to be a quiet leader, and a
master at bringing out the best performance in others, by
improving the way people process information.

*Writing That Works, 3rd Edition: How to Communicate
Effectively in Business*
Kenneth Roman and Joel Raphaelson
This concise, practical guide to the principles of effective
writing contains more than 200 specific examples of
strong e-mails, memos, letters, reports, speeches, and
resumes.

*Errors in English and Ways to Correct Them, 4th Edition:
The Practical Approach to Correct Word Usage, Sentence
Structure, Spelling, Punctuation, and Grammar*
Harry Shaw
This excellent reference guide focuses on some of the
most common errors writers and speakers make and
explains how to correct them with extensive examples
and exercises.

The Elements of Style
William Strunk, Jr., and E. B. White
This best seller, in print since 1957, has instructed
millions on how to write properly, presenting the basics of
composition, grammar, and word usage.

Winning
Jack Welch with Suzy Welch
The core of *Winning* is devoted to the real "stuff" of
work. Packed with personal anecdotes, this book offers
deep insights, original thinking, and solutions to nuts-
and-bolts problems.

On Writing Well: The Classic Guide to Writing Nonfiction
William K. Zinsser
Zinsser's must-read book for anyone who writes on a
daily basis explains the fundamentals of good writing
and advocates a simple, uncluttered, and clear style of
writing.

Index

Make sure you have all the Best Practices!

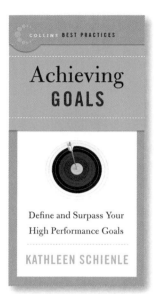

COLLINS BEST PRACTICES

Achieving
GOALS

Define and Surpass Your
High Performance Goals

KATHLEEN SCHIENLE

Best Practices: Achieving Goals
ISBN: 978-0-06-114574-2

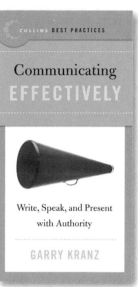

COLLINS BEST PRACTICES

Communicating
EFFECTIVELY

Write, Speak, and Present
with Authority

GARRY KRANZ

Best Practices: Communicating Effectively
ISBN: 978-0-06-114568-1

COLLINS BEST PRACTICES

Difficult
PEOPLE

Working Effectively with
Prickly Bosses, Co-Workers,
and Clients

JOHN HOOVER

Best Practices: Difficult People
ISBN: 978-0-06-114559-9

COLLINS BEST PRACTICES

Evaluating
PERFORMANCE

How to Appraise,
Promote, and Fire

BARRY SILVERSTEIN

Best Practices: Evaluating Performance
ISBN: 978-0-06-114560-5

Make sure you have all the Best Practices!

Best Practices: Managing People
ISBN: 978-0-06-114556-8

Best Practices: Motivating Employees
ISBN: 978-0-06-114561-2

Best Practices: Time Management
ISBN: 978-0-06-114563-6

Best Practices: Hiring People
ISBN: 978-0-06-114557-5